A SOLDIER'S LIFE

THE STORY OF A SOLDIER'S CONSISTENT FAITH AND TRUST IN GOD'S COVENANT PROMISES

AN AUTOBIOGRAPHY BY

R. A. WARD

WESTBOW
PRESS®
A DIVISION OF THOMAS NELSON
& ZONDERVAN

This book is a work of non-fiction. Unless otherwise noted, the author and the publisher make no explicit guarantees as to the accuracy of the information contained in this book and in some cases, names of people and places have been altered to protect their privacy.

WestBow Press books may be ordered through booksellers or by contacting:

WestBow Press
A Division of Thomas Nelson & Zondervan
1663 Liberty Drive
Bloomington, IN 47403
www.westbowpress.com
844-714-3454

Scripture quotations marked KJV are taken from the King James Version.

Scripture quotations marked AMP are taken from the Amplified® Bible, Copyright © 2015 by The Lockman Foundation. Used by permission.

Scripture quotations marked MSG are taken from The Message. Copyright © 1993, 1994, 1995, 1996, 2000, 2001, 2002. Used by permission of NavPress Publishing Group.

Scripture quotations marked CEV are taken from the Contemporary English Version®, Copyright © 1995 American Bible Society. All rights reserved.

ISBN: 978-1-6642-1659-4 (sc)
ISBN: 978-1-6642-1658-7 (hc)
ISBN: 978-1-6642-1660-0 (e)

Library of Congress Control Number: 2020924829

Print information available on the last page.

WestBow Press rev. date: 02/19/2021

CONTENTS

PREFACE

This book contains some of my eye-opening experiences that propelled me from a miracle-based childhood to supernatural experiences during a war-bound, thirty-year career in the US Army. You could call this an incomplete autobiography of one soldier's life of faith in God and His Lord and Savior, Jesus Christ.

From childhood to adulthood, from being single to being married and a father, and to the near-death experiences during combat operations in Iraq, I share these accounts with you in a way I hope will clearly display the true character of God and His divine will for our lives.

This whole journey has been an experience primarily of learning the character of God. If you can identify with others' character, you can discern their intents and purposes, their will, in certain situations and circumstances. You can actually develop a faith in their character. If I spend a great deal of time with a close friend, I would begin to know him or her very well especially if we have been transparent with one another.

As I spend time in God's Word and in prayer, the Holy Spirit guides my steps and reveals to me more of God's will for my life. He hasn't revealed all of what He has purposed for me to be and do, but I will give you an account of my life so far in hopes that you will gain some wisdom from it for the betterment of your life.

This book will confirm what those who know God's character already know about Him. Those who don't have a relationship with

God or are just beginning one with Him will begin to see His will, His Word, and His ways of doing things in accord with the way He's dealt with me. Some of my life's events may set you back on your heels a bit if you have an image of God in your heart different from mine.

The Word of God says in Malachi 3:6, "For I am the Lord, I change not; therefore, ye sons of Jacob are not consumed." His will for mankind has never changed. That's why what He's done to, for, and through me, He'll also do to, for, and through you—if you'll believe.

I hope this book will challenge you to believe and hope in and trust God to levels you've not yet dared to venture. The things that happened in my life caused God's glory to be displayed. They clearly depict God's judgment on certain life matters. Some of these instances were life threatening, but I am still here and whole by the grace of God. I have the privilege of writing my soldier's story, and I urge you to have faith in God for victory and triumph over the many challenges you face today and tomorrow.

CHAPTER 1

IN THE BEGINNING

O ne day in the summer of 1972, when I was five, I got permission to go out and play with the other kids playing in front of my house. As I hippity-hopped down our long driveway, I felt the strong presence of someone going with me. It felt like an adult male, but it wasn't my father. I felt his presence so strongly that he caused me to turn around to see who it was, but there was no one there.

I made it to the sidewalk in front of my house and saw the kids I wanted to play with, but they were at that point across the street, so I started walking across to them. As I got to the middle of the street, a car came flying down the street. All the other kids cleared out of its way, but I didn't see it until it was upon me so close that it should've not only hit me but also launched me a good fifty feet.

Without my making any evasive moves, the car didn't touch me. When it came to a screeching halt, I was lying down under it. I didn't have a scratch. My arms were straight alongside my body as though I were standing at attention, like a soldier. I heard the driver get out of the car and speak frantically to a couple of other parents who came up to the car. I thought, *He's in so much trouble for almost hitting me!* I knew my mom was watching me from the living room window, so I thought, *I'd better get from under here so she doesn't think I'm hurt and make me come inside.* Sure enough, by the time I got out from under there, she was running across the street.

I wondered how I had gotten under there without having been hurt at all. Once I started moving, I was scratched by things on the ground, and the car's exhaust pipe burned my arm when I tried to roll over to get out. I wondered how I had ended up under the car without it touching me, and then I knew it was the presence that had followed me outside that day that had ensured my safety. I began to learn about angels.

Two years later, in 1974, my father and mother gave their lives to the Lord, and that's when all our lives really began to change. Normally, I would see my father get up in the morning and smoke a cigarette to start his day, but the day after he gave his life to the Lord, when he lit up, he began to gag as though he had never smoked before. He never smoked another cigarette. Their giving their lives to the Lord changed the atmosphere in my home for everyone.

Soon after their day of salvation came a day when I changed in ways my parents did not realize. A few months after that day in 1974 (I was seven then), I had also given my life to the Lord and was baptized.[1] When I went under in that water for the baptism, it felt like an eternity and as if I had been teleported to some other place in the universe, but when I came out, I knew something was different. I knew I was not the same. The ministers and my dad would've done well to explain to me the strange things that would happen because of my baptism. With receiving no explanation and being asked to speak in that same unknown language I heard my parents speaking,[2] I refused to open my mouth. My tongue was twisting around inside, and I knew that if I opened my mouth to say anything, it was not going to sound like English. So I kept my lips together tightly.

After that day, my father introduced me to the Bible. At age seven, I had real difficulty understanding the King James Version. After I read something in it, my father would have me explain what I had read. At first, I couldn't really explain to him anything I had read, but when he applied the rule of not being able to go outside and play, I concentrated on the scriptures. Still not understanding the thuses and thous of the King James Version, I heard it plainly in me, *Thou means you.* I immediately knew within me that it was the truth. I wasn't sure who was talking to me, but I felt He was present and going over the scriptures with me just like my parents would help me with homework.[3] I began to expect that voice to speak to me and give me understanding whenever I read the Bible.

In 1974, my father, who had worked at a manufacturing plant for the previous thirteen years, found himself unemployed due to the economic downturn sweeping the nation. But I also began to watch him exercise his faith in God, and what I saw shifted my outlook on what I thought it meant to be a Christian.

One afternoon, after playing football with my friends, I began to get hungry. I went home and asked my mother for a snack, but she said I'd have to wait for dinner. When she said that, something went off inside me like an explosion. I didn't understand what it was, so I disregarded the alarm her words gave me. She said I should drink some water. I looked in the refrigerator for cold water, but the refrigerator was empty. I turned to tell my mom what she already knew about the fridge, but instead, I continued to survey the kitchen. To my surprise, the entire kitchen was bare as well. My mom wasn't preparing to cook anything, but yet, she was standing at the stove as if to do so. *What's going on?* I wondered.

At that moment, my father walked into the kitchen and spoke. For the first time, I heard words of faith spoken in our home, words that had a real impact on me. My mother's words had made me pause, but when my father spoke, his words filled the room; I was assured that what he said was true. I forgot my hunger; I just wanted to get back out to play some more.

What he said to me wasn't way out there like a Nostradamus prophesy, but it calmed my hunger. Without having heard me ask my mother for a snack, he said, "Man! We're going to eat good tonight!" I didn't question that at all; his words went into me as if they were the snack I was looking for. It was just a basic statement, but it was full of power. He believed it, and he spoke it;[4] as it is written in 2 Corinthians 4:13, "We have the same spirit of faith, according as it is written, I believed, and therefore have I spoken; we also believe, and therefore speak." I believed my father's belief, so I knew I was hearing the truth and received it in heart as truth. My father was my shepherd, so I followed him as he followed Christ.

As an adult, I now know of plenty scriptures he could've hung his faith on, but the one that comes to mind at this moment is Psalm 37:25, "*I have been young, and now am old; yet have I not seen the righteous forsaken, nor his seed begging bread.*"

He had been studying the Bible all that morning, and whatever he read out of God's Word had lit a fire in him; he would not accept anything less than what the Bible said. This man of God declared, "Man! We're going to eat good tonight." Job 22:28 reads, "*Thou shalt also decree a thing, and it [meaning what you have decreed in line with God's Word] shall be established unto thee: and the light shall shine upon thy ways.*"

Psalm 37:25 tells of God's character toward His people. And when you confess God's Word concerning your situation or circumstance, it's as though you have a water hose with a kink in it; the water's on full blast but nothing's coming out on your end. But when you make your decree in line with what He said about it in His Word, you unkink the hose and what God has had for you all along makes its way into your life full force. I don't know if my father knew what he was doing, but that day, his belief in God's Word gave him the confidence to make that declaration.

When I went home that evening, there wasn't anything prepared for dinner. The kitchen looked the same as it did when I had been there a few hours earlier. I asked my mom what we were having for dinner, and she said, "I don't know, but we'll have something, so get cleaned up."

She had me set the table for the three of us. That was unusual as we had never done that before, but I remembered my father saying that we would eat well that night, so I held onto his word because not having food had never been an issue in our home before.

At six, my father came into the kitchen. I still saw no evidence that we were going to have dinner. My father seemed unconcerned, so I was unconcerned as well. He told me that the table looked good and that I should sit in his seat at the head of the table, which was a high honor indeed. We all sat. He extended his hands to me and my mom and said, "Let's give thanks." He said, "Lord, we give thanks for the—"

He was interrupted by a knock on the door, and he got up to answer it. It was our neighbor, who was holding a huge commercial pot. He said, "I hope you haven't cooked yet. I cooked way too much tonight."

My dad calmly said, "No, we haven't cooked anything yet." Our neighbor offered us some stuffed pasta shells with his special sauce and homemade French bread, and then he asked my father to come to his house for a lot more pasta and bread. He and my father went to his house, and they returned with two more pots and plenty more bread.

The amount of food he gave us made me wonder what he had been thinking when he prepared all that food. He wasn't married and had no children. He was a mechanic by trade, but he was well known for his skills as a chef, and he cooked for restaurants of the highest caliber in our city. Every day after he closed his shop, he cooked. The other kids and I would feast off the aromas coming out of his kitchen window; they would prompt us to run home and ask our parents what they were making for dinner.

But his bringing us that much food was very unusual. My parents asked him to stay for supper, and he came into our home for the first time and ate with us. The food was fantastic as my father had said it would be. As we ate, my father told him about his belief that God would provide food for his family because there was none. Our neighbor explained why he had cooked so much. He said that everything he measured out caused an abundance of food. When he was all done, he had filled his largest pots and had nowhere else to put it all. Then my father explained salvation to him, how God loved him, and how He wanted him to turn his life over to Him so He could do something better with it. Our neighbor said that he already had that unction in his heart before that day and that he was ready. They prayed the prayer of salvation at our kitchen table.

It took us three days to eat all that food, and it was good every day. Our neighbor's business boomed, and he finally got married. I was just a child, but I was so happy for him and his wife, who was very nice and pretty. Her inner beauty loved on all the kids. She was such a great addition to our neighborhood. All this happened on the heels of my father's decree, "We're going to eat good tonight." Before then, our neighbor did not know our financial situation. Not once had he come into our home. Plus, my father was not the type to make his personal business known to others. This neighbor had watched as we drove around in our big Cadillac and saw my father host parties. His having said that had he hoped that we hadn't cooked yet led me to believe that he hadn't been aware of our situation.

I reviewed the chain of events that day and everything my parents had said and concluded that only God could've orchestrated an outcome like that. I'd read about God splitting the Red Sea for the Israelites when they were facing certain death from the Egyptian army in Exodus 14:15–31 and how David, at age seventeen, had killed Goliath with the empowerment of God in 1 Samuel 17. I was sure God had done that for us though it seemed to be a much smaller deed by comparison. I also identified with the formula or blueprint of faith my father lived by. My father exercised his faith, trust, and unrelenting confidence in God, and the truth of God's Word became a reality before my eyes.

This unforgettable event became my first foundational reference point of walking by faith. I understood that if I believed the Word of God, my actions had to coincide with that belief. My father's belief in God's Word had caused him to act a certain way and speak certain things that day. He didn't do things that reflected disbelief such as asking someone for food or conducting himself in a way that would have given anyone an indication that our cupboards might have been bare.

I grew up in the origins of the hip-hop era. One thing that was the backbone of that genre and preached in the playgrounds and in the streets of my youth was, "Be about what you believe!" If others wanted to know what you stood for, they needed only to watch you operate. That was also the only way anyone around my neighborhood would believe anything you said. No one believed what you said if they didn't see it in your conduct first. Watching my father walk out the blueprint of faith forever solidified in my heart what Christian conduct was for me. It was not based on any religious factors. My father told me, "You have to know God and His Word for yourself! Don't rely solely on a pastor, church, or visiting preacher to come to town and teach you!" That hit me like a ton of bricks.

Something dramatically shifted in me. His words seemed to edit my genome and reset my standards of conduct. I understood at that moment that God's intent was to have a one-on-one, intimate relationship with me and everyone else for that matter. Studying His Word is how you begin to know Him and His ways.

I believe that my father doing the Word, not just hearing it, was the key to his receiving the biblical results he obtained as a believer. James 1:22 says, "But be ye doers of the word, and not hearers only, deceiving your own selves."

I resolved to cooperate in faith with God's Word. I navigate life based on the legacy of faith I received from my father. Even at a young age, I perceived this to be a commandment, not a negotiable approach to life for believers. When I study something in the Word and act on it in faith, biblical results happen for me and my family.

CHAPTER 2

THE BEGINNING OF A LIFE OF FAITH

The Lord has shown me a great many things He had in store for me, many of which have already manifested. But nothing transformed my life of faith more profoundly than when He showed me my future wife and children in a vision. (More about that in chapter 6). There's no way of explaining it other than as an inward knowing of it being the truth. Some would ask why the Lord would reveal that to me instead of something more suitable for a child my age. I believe He intended His revelation to anchor my faith at that time in my life and give me hope for my future.

I was only nine then, but I had already given my life to the Lord. Despite what some adult Christians around me believed about children in those days, I had been baptized at my request and knew I was filled with the Holy Spirit. From that moment on, my thoughts and outlook about many things changed.

FAITH STUFF

In 1974, when I was seven, faith stuff began happening in my house after my parents turned their lives over to the Lord. I witnessed and understood some deeper things in the Word of God because something was beginning to make what I heard and saw understandable.

Other kids were sent to different parts of the church to play while their parents heard the Word of God in the sanctuary. My father insisted that I sit with them with my Bible and listen to what was being taught or spoken about. I began to grow in knowledge and understanding. I was still just a kid and acted like one, but I was maturing spiritually and learning some things in the Bible that the other kids weren't.

My father instituted Bible study time for me, which generally meant that my face was going to be deeply planted in Proverbs for at least an hour each time. Getting permission to go play depended on whether the comprehensive report I gave my dad was acceptable.

When I was nine, I had gotten away from studying the Word because my father went away to Bible college and my mother did not enforce my Bible study time. I soon found myself hanging around others who had poor reputations. Within a few months, I was going right along with them and doing the things they did instead of doing what I knew was right. In time, I lost sight of the case study of myself I was conducting in my mind. My research at that time was not complete. It seemed that whenever I did something wrong with other kids, I was the only one to be caught and punished. One time, when I was nine, I found myself in the back seat of a police car. I had been caught stealing around three o'clock that afternoon in a park far from my home, where I had gone without my mother's permission. When the policeman released us, I was so afraid of what my mother would do that I didn't go straight home. Around midnight, my cousin found me at a neighbor's house and brought me home. I thought, *I'm going to be grounded for the rest of the summer and get a spanking on top of that!*

I slowly walked into my house and saw my mom. Instead of scolding and punishing me, she just looked me over for a few seconds and then walked to her bedroom. Her hurt and fear for my well-being was overwhelming. It was as though I had caused her to age ten years in just nine hours. Seeing my mother's hurt and disappointment was worse than any spanking I could've gotten; it was like getting a hundred lashes to my heart. I was not pleased with myself for having allowed someone to talk me into doing something I knew was wrong, and I felt great shame for embarrassing my mom in front of our family and neighbors. Within hours, everyone knew what her son had done while her husband was away. I vowed I'd never bring shame on my family like that again.

The next morning, I woke up to my name being called from the sidewalk outside. It was my aunt, the oldest of my mother's sisters. I still don't know if she had volunteered her services or if my mother had called her in. Even I knew that I deserved punishment. I was hoping just this one time that we could forgo any traditional punishment, but my aunt brought all her spanking skills to bear on me. At least I wasn't restricted to the house as my father would have ruled for violations of family rules and values to reset my behavior concerning my lying, stealing, disobeying my parents, and not being home on time, the rules I had broken.

He thought that restricting me to the house or yard would ensure that what had happened would not happen again, but my mother skipped the restriction part. I actually missed my father's leadership at that moment. Weird, huh? Rendering punishment was something my mother hadn't been responsible for in some time; Pop handled discipline matters in the family. I knew that not being restricted would create a huge problem for me with the other kids; the others received no punishment from their parents even though the policeman had spoken to them while we sat in the back of the patrol car. Thank God the man whose item we stole convinced the policeman to forget the whole thing.

I realized it wasn't good for me to hang around those other kids any longer; I'd have to publicly break free of them. I knew which kids to play with and which I should not play with, but I was forced to confront this unhealthy relationship alone. I knew that without my father there to protect me and tell me what I could and couldn't do, I was destined to find myself in even deeper trouble if I continued to hang around with the wrong kids. So I put myself on restriction as I thought my father would have. I knew it would be at least six months before I would see him again. I decided that the so-called friendships I had were not worth all the trouble they could get me in.

All we ever did was steal. Whenever we went to a store, something was always stolen. One day, I bought some candy at the corner store because I wanted some and had the money for it. When the others saw me actually buy the candy, they criticized me all the way back to the neighborhood for that. We hardly ever played for the fun of it. If we rode our bicycles around, it was only to scout out what we could steal. Even the bike they let me ride was a compilation of stolen parts. I made a vow that night never do those things I had done ever again.

Shortly after my self-restriction, the kids came over to my house and said, "Come on! Let's go!" I felt pressured; I felt that I was at the edge of a dark pit and that if I took another step, I'd fall in and never get out of it. I was angry that they didn't seem to care about me or my future. I told them, "I'm not going anywhere! I got in trouble, and I'm not getting in trouble again." They began to threaten me and bully me. I told them that I wasn't afraid of them and was prepared to fight whoever stepped up. No one had the courage to challenge me in that area. They never bothered me again.

I sat on my porch and wondered, *What am I going to do and be when I grow up?* I knew that if I continued down the path I had been on, I would end up where I didn't want to be. Just then, the Holy Spirit (though I didn't know Him) gave me a vision of a beautiful woman whose face was blurred and young boys. That took me aback. I sensed I was being shown that I would be a husband and father. I was thrust into the future, where they existed. I was observing them, but they were not aware of that. I was greatly uplifted. As I accepted this vision as my future, an indescribable fire entered my heart along with a heightened level of maturity and awareness. I began to look at my life based on what the Holy Spirit had shown me; that woman and those boys were in my mind in everything I thought of doing from then on.

The Holy Spirit had shown me my future wife, and I knew we would be exact fits for each other. He had shown me the boys I would raise and teach with God's guidance; I would point them to their destinies.[1] Since we were having such a great conversation, I asked the Holy Spirit why I was always told to be quiet, to shut up, and that I didn't know what I was talking about. He didn't give me an explanation; He simply said, "One day, everybody will listen to you." At a time of feeling pretty low about myself, that was exactly what I needed to hear. What that encounter with the Holy Spirit did for me that day still resonates in me more than forty years later.

CHAPTER 3

FROM DEATH TO LIFE BY USING YOUR MEASURE OF FAITH

When I was young boy, I watched my mother's belly growing when she was pregnant. The time she was pregnant with her fifth child was the most challenging. While she was pregnant, my dad began disappearing more and more into his room in the evenings. Because of our growing family, the home we lived in eventually became short on private space, so it was very hard for any of us to find time alone.

I asked my mom why Dad would go to their bedroom at the time we would all normally be watching television together. She told me that he was fasting and what fasting was all about,[1] but she didn't explain why my father was fasting.

I found out why he had been fasting the day he returned from the hospital without the traditional report about a new baby. My sister had been born dead, and my mother had almost died in the process. Let me tell you this story of extraordinary faith.

My father told me that satan had told him and Mom that he would kill my unborn sister and mother. Of course my father rebuked that, but he also began to fast and study the Word to find what God had said concerning such attacks by the enemy. He discovered the promises of God for life, and for weeks before the delivery, he meditated on them in the same way the Lord told Joshua in Joshua 1:8–9.

This book of the law shall not depart out of thy mouth; but thou shalt meditate therein day and night, that thou mayest observe to do according to all that is written therein: for then thou shalt make thy way prosperous, and then thou shalt have good success. Have not I commanded thee? Be strong and of a good courage; be not afraid, neither be thou dismayed: for the Lord thy God is with thee whithersoever thou goest.

He meditated on the Word of God to the point that His promises were as agreeable to his soul as the answer to the equation 2 + 2 was. I call this executing a faith operation. I'm talking about someone sowing a seed—the word of faith from scriptures—into his or her heart and reaping a physical harvest much as farmers do[3] or like my two youngest boys who brought their seed projects home from school to show us. I think we all had such seed projects in grade school; we planted seeds and followed our teachers' instructions, which were on point I learned when I saw the results in fourth grade of those who had followed the teacher's instructions and those who had not and ended up begging for another seed because theirs had not sprouted. I was among them because I hadn't understood the importance of following instructions.

My father knew that following God's instructions was his only option for overcoming the enemy's attack. The true motivator for him I believe was that he knew victory was already his, that he simply needed to find the promise in the Word that would confirm it and then meditate it and speak words according to it until it manifested.

A FATHER'S TRANSFERRING OF FAITH

The day my mother and father prepared to go to the hospital, my eyes were fixed on him. He exuded confidence, strength, and courage but also peace. As they left, my father told me that they were going to deliver the baby and he'd be back after that.

I knew that his words were very important. He taught me through his actions to be very choice with my words while on the battlefield of faith, but I don't think he realized that he was teaching me then. He had meditated on the Word of God for so long that the seed of the Word had grown into a tree inside him. He left me the fruit of love for my family, joy that the day had finally come for my sister to be born, inner peace that there wouldn't be any problems, faith in him because he was walking out his faith in God, and temperance to be responsible for my siblings and exercise the leadership required while my parents were gone. He fed me fruit from the tree that had matured within him.

How ironic is it that young children would rather eat from their parents' plates than their own. I believe that children eat from the spiritual plates of their parents as well. They watch their parents' every move and hang on their words. Even when it looks as if they're not paying attention to their parents, they're perceiving their parents' thoughts and interpreting their countenances. They eat what their parents feed them including their attitudes, beliefs, fears, and so on because they are their parents. Even when they seem to reject what their parents would feed them, their parents will later find out that they had indeed digested it. That day, my father left me with enough of what he filled me with to feed my brothers and sister. I had no problems with them the entire night.

MANIFESTATION OF THE UNBELIEVABLE

As the enemy had foretold, there were complications with the baby before she was born. She wasn't breathing or moving. The ultrasound showed the umbilical cord wrapped around her neck. They got her out as fast as they could, but she was dead. The doctor and nurses tried to resuscitate her, but she did not respond. Then my mom began having complications. My father did not tell me exactly what happened to my mom, but everyone in the delivery room turned their full attention to her. They stabilized her, but the new baby was lost. After they attempted to console him, my father told everyone to get out of the delivery room. They left my parents and the baby in the room. Remembering his covenant rights and authority over all the power of the enemy, my father called life by my sister's name back into her body in Jesus's name, and my sister started crying. As Jesus said in Luke 10:19, *"Behold, I give unto you power to tread on serpents and scorpions, and over all the power of the enemy: and nothing shall by any means hurt you."*

My sister had been born dead. She had not breathed for six minutes. As my father told me about this, I imagined the frantic actions of the nurses as they rushed back into the room and began to handle this newborn who had been visibly and clinically dead the last time they had seen her. They asked my father, "What happened? How is the baby breathing?"

Knowing that my father was always brash and bold about what he believed, I identified with the dominating force of faith coming from him as he retold the encounter. He had a new, overwhelming confidence in God and His Word. My faith in God was greatly impacted in that moment. This was not a story written in the Bible; this was happening in my personal life. My father had imparted to me such a trust and confidence that from that point on, my outlook has never been the same. By his faithful conduct, he solidified the foundation of faith in me, at age twelve, that he had begun some five years earlier. It's this same lineage of faith I now impart to my sons today.

He told me that the hospital would be keeping my mother and sister for three days to make sure they were fit to come home. I understood that. But there was still no clinical explanation for how a baby who had been pronounced dead was not only alive but also well.

Three days later, my father brought my mother home; my sister stayed there for three more days and further tests. The doctors said that the lack of oxygen she had experienced might affect her motor skills such as walking and talking and cognitive reasoning and memory. To me, that sounded like a smart way to say she would be a vegetable! I considered my baby sister as a hostage kept at the hospital against the wishes of her parents and family. The battle was on!

SCENT OF WAR

When Dad felt that he had been forced to accept the situation, the atmosphere in our home shifted. I watched him closely to see which way he had judged the situation in his heart. It was not long before my countenance became the same as his. I set aside the joy I felt for my sister's being alive and focused just on her coming home. At age twelve, I knew nothing of the protocol hospitals exercised when faced with such circumstances, and I didn't care. I knew only that my sister was alive and that the doctors hadn't a thing negative to say about her condition as a newborn; they only speculated about her future. As I saw it, no one offered my father any legitimate reason why she shouldn't be brought home the same way the rest of us were when we were born. Having this conversation about my new sister with my father caused me to believe that my righteous indignation was in line with his.

I was experiencing for the first time what I call the scent of war. That's an atmosphere found only on and synonymous with the field of battle. It brings about a steely-eyed focus on victory over whatever stands in your way—a singular point of thought. Even now, at the point of every attack of the enemy on me, my family, or anyone in my purview, this battlefield aroma presents itself. It determines my level of focus and strengthens my resolve to gain uncompromised victory. In these moments, no other outcome is acceptable.

My father prepped the battlefield long before the day of my sister's delivery having had foreknowledge of what the enemy would attempt on that fateful day, but I don't believe he thought the battle would go this far. For days after the first three, my dad went back and forth to the hospital demanding that his daughter be released to him. On the ninth day, he was notified by the hospital that a court order had been granted to the hospital for temporary custody of his daughter to squelch his attempts to collect her.

My father said that a campaign had been launched to remove all my parents' children from their custody in addition to the temporary custody order. I did not know exactly what that meant, and he wouldn't go any deeper into explaining it, but I perceived that my dad had a real fight on his hands.

The court hearing was set for the eighteenth day after my sister's birth. The court hearing, I believe, was to be a formal notification to my father that he would lose custody of his child.

For this man of God, that was what you call the moment of truth. For all that he professed and confessed as a Christian in faith to those who did not believe, the monumental moment was upon him to stand tall and unwavering. This was the day of judgment when justice would be found. He would have to show up on the battlefield to see the truth of God's Word manifest. This moment was the pinnacle of walking by faith. It's the moment when you decide that you're going to stick with God and His Word. Everything was hanging on this one decision. If my father backed off, it would've ensured his defeat and probably enabled the complete disbanding of his family. He had nowhere to go but with God, so my father stayed in faith, and we were all in agreement with him.

In the face of your toughest trial in life, will you dare to have faith in God,[7] or will you bow your knee? Every believer must answer that question when faced with adversity. Some might believe they aren't required to answer adversity, "just be quiet and it'll go away", but there's a greater opportunity for loss and defeat if you don't stand up and answer the opposing force. If you fight this good fight of faith even when it looks like all is lost, your victory will manifest.[6] I've been the victor too many times on so many challenging levels to say that walking by faith and fighting the good fight doesn't work because it does for those who have faith in God.[7]

My father took nothing but his Bible into the courtroom that day. I do not know what my father said or read out of the Bible, but whatever he did or said made the judge say, "Get your baby and get out of here! Case closed!"

Eighteen days after that faith-filled day in the delivery room, my dad was finally bringing his daughter home, and I was finally able to meet whom this great battle had been fought and won for. At the impressionable age of twelve, I realized that the Lord took this opportunity to instill in me the principal example of how to fight the good fight of faith. I also understood that there's a level of uncompromised tenacity required to fight the good fight.

The enemy will try to heap enough pressure on you to convince you to cower and back off your faith in God's Word. Trust me! Cultivate the uncompromising tenacity my father displayed through this ordeal. I watched my father work kingdom principles and be successful at it. This great victory continues to be my measuring tool for how far I believe God will go with us if we dare to show up and do battle His way. My father went into the jaws of death and got his daughter back. This to me could not have been a more fitting example of having faith and trust in God. In Mark 11:22, Jesus said plainly, "Have faith in God."

The key takeaway I got from my father's trek through this faith operation was that he believed and used nothing but the Word of God to take dominion over the situation, and it didn't cost him a dime.[4] He didn't have to get a lawyer, and most important to me in my own faith walk, he did not bow to the powers that be. He simply applied the Word in faith as the Holy Spirit instructed him to. When all seemed lost, he stood on God's Word and was not in doubt with his fingers crossed behind his back.

This battle was a battle for the right to live and a battle for a man to maintain the right to raise his children according to God's divine instruction, not according to the dictates of society. Because of this, my father received what God promised in His Word: victory, not defeat. Triumph, not continued adversity. I was privileged to watch the process. On that day, I had in my arms the manifested truth of what my father had been saying to me. I then understood why I had to have faith in God and why we all must live by that same faith in Him. Fighting the good fight requires it. It's not a good fight if your faith in God's Word isn't being exercised. Believing and doing what the Word says will ensure your victory in every fight.

That fight of faith takes place daily. Make no mistake about that. Your faith in God is challenged every day. Just think about it for a moment; you are in this world but not of it, right? Jesus said in John 17:14, *"I have given them thy word; and the world hath hated them, because they are not of the world, even as I am not of the world."*

If you're not of the world but in it, that means you and everything about you is contrary to this world. Those who don't understand this or disagree with it easily succumb to the demands and pressures of this world either deliberately or unaware. In either case, they won't know how to resist or don't believe they can or should resist in days like the ones my father had to stand in. I'm not trying to offend anyone; I'm trying to provoke others to see what I'm saying in hope that they will desire the liberty that fighting the good fight of faith brings. No resistance, no victory! This is how so many of my brothers and sisters in Christ have lived lives way below the quality they could be living and have allowed injustices to persist in their lives without saying a word. I've watched this play out in the lives of so many all over the nation and from varied walks of life. My compassion for them all is overwhelming. I want people to be free from whatever prohibits them from soaring in their lives. Having faith in God and acting on His words of promise can change everything in your life for the better. Having faith in God makes room for His ability to operate in our lives for our good. My father gave Him room, and he was victorious.

CHAPTER 4

CONTINUING TO GROW FROM FAITH TO FAITH

I n my teen years, I was exposed to a few things that caused me to doubt Christianity, but my knowing that God was alive and ever present was never in question. The problem was that I allowed other Christians' conduct to sour my zeal for the things of God. When I should've held tight to the one-on-one relationship I had with God, I allowed the enticement of the things of the world to cause me to journey further and further from Him.

In 1981, I began to hang around older teenagers who introduced me to marijuana. In 1983, I began consuming alcohol. That caused years of rebellion against my parents to the point that they worried about me even when sending me to the local grocery store. I had allowed my life to get so off base that I often asked myself why I couldn't tell my parents the truth when they asked for it. I was so afraid of their knowing what I had been doing that I piled lie on top of lie.

One day, my father asked me to go to the post office for a roll of stamps. When I got home, I put the stamps, the receipt, and the change on the kitchen counter and went to bed. The next morning, he woke me up and asked about the stamps, and I told him they were on the kitchen counter. Later that morning, my mother also asked me about the stamps, and I gave her the same answer. I realized that the questioning wasn't really about the stamps; it was about my repeated violations of their trust. I understood that their distrust of me was warranted and that I had no right to be offended by their questioning.

They could not find the stamps or the change that I had brought home. I tried to convince them to believe me, but my mother yelled, "You're a liar! I don't believe you!" My heart was crushed. She had been my unconditional supporter. I couldn't explain what had happened to the items after I had put them on the counter. After they finished their inquiry, I was released to go and wash up for breakfast. I was deeply hurt by what had been said, and I was baffled about what had happened to the stamps.

My father came into the bathroom and had some additional words with me that cut even deeper. But while he was berating me, my mother yelled out that she had found the stamps, the receipt, and the change in the trashcan in the kitchen. My father remembered that they had been teaching my three-year-old sister to put trash in the trashcan to help Mom in the kitchen. They figured that she must have thought the stamps were trash and put them in the trashcan along with the receipt and change.

My father apologized for what he had said to me, but I'd been so hurt by his words that I didn't know how to respond. Mixed emotions had me feeling worthy of the ridicule and damaged in my heart. I realized that if I hadn't been so deceitful in the past, maybe it wouldn't have been so easy for them to disbelieve me. I was very hurt and didn't want to feel that way again, so I avoided verbal punishments like that by continuing to cover for the things I had done in the recent past with more lies.

In 1987, at twenty years of age, I joined the army. After graduating from basic training and advanced individual training, I began to drink alcohol regularly. The first social introduction I got from a group of noncommissioned officers (NCOs) was how to drink an excessive amount of hard liquor. They called it teaching me the ropes.

The lessons continued up to the point that I took the reins and began to instruct myself in this manner. Within a year, I became a prime example of an alcohol abuser. I was leading a riotous life, which was a cultural norm for most young soldiers then. I was a good and disciplined soldier while in uniform and most respectful when conducting myself in public, but my alcohol consumption was getting out of hand. Not a day went by that I didn't drink.

THE MIRACLE

Two years after joining my first unit, I received my orders for reassignment to a unit overseas. That would be the first time I lived in another country and the first time I would be without those who had taught me my new tricks. I took some vacation time and visited my family. I ran into an old friend and convinced him to come back to where I was stationed and stay with me for a week.

During that time, I showed him one of the new tricks I had learned with alcohol—drinking and driving. My leadership had drilled into our minds the dangers of drinking and driving, but this one particular night, I didn't calculate things very well. I thought that my friend would be able to drive my car if I drank too much. After having what we called a good time, we decided to leave the establishment and go to my unit to sleep it off.

When we got to my barracks, the sergeant on duty would not allow my friend to stay because he was a civilian. The only option I had was to drive to my girlfriend's house, but the effects of the alcohol had really set in. I asked my friend to drive, but to my surprise, he said he didn't know how to drive a five-speed manual shift and didn't have a driver's license.

As intoxicated as I was, I decided to drive to my girlfriend's house. I was fading fast and wasn't sure if I could make it, but something said to me, *You're a soldier! If you've marched hundreds of miles with a rucksack on your back, surely you can do this too!* I felt I was being set up, but I took the challenge. I figured that if I drove out the back gate, I could avoid the military police and be miles closer to getting to her house. I had only about five minutes before the MPs would lock that gate for the night. As I turned the last corner to reach the gate, I ran right into the MPs giving everyone Breathalyzer tests. *This isn't happening!* I thought. I thought about backing out of line, but that would've surely drawn the attention I was seeking to avoid.

I was stuck. The only thing I could do to avoid a bad-conduct discharge was to pass the Breathalyzer test. As the MP approached my car, something came over me. I instantly sobered up. Out of nowhere, my demeanor and faculties were as though I hadn't drunk a thing. Something was happening to me that I had never felt before, but I had no time to figure it out. Nor was I going to explain it to the MP, who was at that point knocking on my window. I rolled the window down, and the MP asked me if I had been drinking. I told him yes, that my friend had had such a great time that he couldn't drive. I lied; I told him I had kept my drinking under the limit as I was the designated driver. I explained that I was being reassigned overseas and that I had brought my friend up to the installation to have a few drinks with me before I left.

The officer told me that he would have to test me, but they were having a problem with the Breathalyzer. He had me step out of the car to test my motor skills. Not feeling intoxicated anymore gave me the courage to comply with a good attitude. My balance was impeccable. I even shocked myself. The officer, being pleased with my performance, let us pass through the gate.

Feeling miraculously sober and being outside the direct jurisdiction of the military, I thought I'd make it to my destination safely. But about a quarter-mile past the gate, all the symptoms of being totally drunk came upon me again. I couldn't believe it. I was afraid. I was unable to keep the car on my side of the road, and I had a hard time keeping a grip on the steering wheel; my hand kept falling off. I fought to keep my eyes open and stay conscious. The highway was a major thoroughfare for eighteen-wheelers, and they were blowing my little car around making it even harder for me to keep it on the road. I was in deep trouble.

I thought about getting off the road, but there were no roads that crossed that highway for the next ten miles. I wanted to just pull off the road, but the road was elevated, and I couldn't pull over without flipping the car. I was stuck on that road and fading fast. I felt we were not going to make it. I looked to my friend for help, but he was in a deep sleep. I had never been more afraid in my life. Believing that I couldn't stay conscious any longer and staring at the center of the steering wheel instead of the road, I cried out, "God! Help me!"[1] I fell unconscious.

As I regained consciousness, I opened my eyes (with my heart pounding so hard that I could count the beats at the top of my throat) and looked at my friend, who was still asleep. My car was still running. I felt okay and began to be thankful, but there was one problem. We were no longer on the highway. I looked in every direction to see nothing but pitch-black darkness. Only the light coming from my headlights gave any indication of where we might be. My joy began to fade.

Where are we? I thought. I'm a fan of the original Star Trek, a real trekkie, so a few sci-fi ideas ran through my mind. I opened the door and peeked out. I saw ground. I put a foot on it. It felt solid, so I got out and stepped into the illumination of the headlights hoping to determine where we were. The most important thing was known, though—We weren't dead. The fact that I could still hear my friend's heavy snoring assured me of that.

I assessed that we were in a field of some sort. *But where's the highway?* I wondered. We'd been on the highway the last time I remembered. I didn't know what direction to go in to reach the highway. I looked in every direction for anything that would tell me where we were, but there wasn't any light anywhere except for my headlights.

I heard a long, low-volume, hissing sound in the distance. I turned in the direction of that sound. If it hadn't been as quiet out there as it was, I wouldn't have heard the sound. I saw what appeared to be the headlights of an eighteen-wheeler in the distance. That told me how far we were from the highway. My car was parallel to it and facing the same direction we had been traveling when we were on it. I had some questions. *How did we get all the way out here so far away from the highway without our being aware of it? Why is my car parallel to the highway instead of facing away from it? And why are we not dead?*

Being thankful that we were alive and knowing which direction to go in, I hopped back in the car to get back to the highway. I noticed how extremely unfriendly the ground was. It was obvious that we were in a field that had been prepared for planting, and I had to drive across the deeply dug rows to get back to the highway. The thought that I had been the one who drove the car to where we ended up in that field was ludicrous to me. How could I have navigated that steep embankment just right to keep the car from flipping over? The terrain was so terrible going back to the highway that it felt like it was damaging my car's suspension. It took about ten minutes to get back to the highway, and then I had to drive up the steep incline at a weird angle just to get back on it again.

Using the off-road training techniques I had learned with Humvees, I managed to climb back onto the highway and make it to the house. All the while, I racked my brain over the whole ordeal. I am convinced that there was no possible way that I had gotten us out of danger, off that highway without flipping the car over, and across that unforgiveable terrain that far away from the highway all while unconscious and under the influence of alcohol.

I never told anyone about that night. Not even my friend, who didn't wake up until we were back on the highway. I believed that whomever I told might have called me a liar or even crazy simply because I was alive to tell the story. There's no way we should've survived.

I no longer rack my brain about how I survived the incident. I know that God heard me when I asked for Him to help me.[1] I believed God's Word long ago when I read Romans 10:13: *"For whosoever shall call upon the name of the Lord shall be saved."*

My prayer activated the ability of my angel who had saved me before to save me again that night.[2] I couldn't believe that I had saved us. All glory must go to my Father, God, for His mercy. Without it, my short life would've been over that night. My death would have affected the lives of so many, and they would not have gotten the chance to know me as they do today. And the seed of all my children would have died with me. I wouldn't have been in my wife's life at the times she needed me the most. Life as I and my family know it today would not exist.

I marvel at the fruit of my salvation. The hand of God is present in everything I see and do today. My sons are accustomed to being stared at by me, and they know I love them. Every day, I am reminded about the goodness God has shown me. Just their existence alone is a testament to the fact that He is good.

I didn't meet my wife until five years after the car miracle, but I still hadn't changed my ways. It wasn't until six years after that night that I quit drinking. Some of us have to reach rock bottom before we will adjust our priorities in life.

CHAPTER 5

THE LOST YEAR

I have met so many people who in many different ways have said, "If I had only known what I know now about life, I would have done a lot of things differently." Are you one of them? Do you soberly, without emotion or excuse, acknowledge your moments of poor judgment? Were or are you willing to make tough decisions to get your life back on track regardless of how you'd look in the eyes of others or what it would mean to your socioeconomic status?

As a young man of twenty-two in 1990, I thought I knew better than anyone else what was best for me. I'd often ignore others' advice because I thought I knew better than those who had already gained wisdom in some critical areas of life including finances and relationships.

I met a young lady who had grown up in a small town not far from my military base. The advice she commonly received from friends and family was to stay clear of soldiers from the base; she told me that when I was developing an interest in her and wanted to get to know her better. I began to wonder if she could possibly be the one I'd been looking for; the one I saw in my vision.

After three months of spending time with her, I acknowledged that I had met a very nice person but not the one. However, I wanted to dispel the myth that soldier boys were not to be trusted, so instead of ending the relationship as I should have, I asked her to marry me. I didn't want to give her friends the satisfaction of rubbing it in her face that they had been right.

The date was set, and we were going to get married without the blessing or agreement of our parents or friends. She knew that her parents would never consent to it, and I didn't know what my parents would say about it, so I decided to call them to find out.

Thankfully, my mother answered the phone. Knowing all along that I was doing the wrong thing, I didn't believe that I could handle my father's putting the truth in my face. For whatever reason, we were having trouble with our long-distance connection. All she heard was that I was getting married. Before the connection was lost, I heard her say, "Son, don't do it!" She had an unction that I was about to make the wrong decision. I realized that if she wasn't in favor of the marriage, I could rest assured that my father wasn't either. I had my answer.

She and I never spoke of the lack of support from our families, but not having it affected our relationship deeply. We didn't understand how important the blessings of our parents were. On our day, I was so out of sorts that I had to drink something just to be able to go through with it. I knew deep down that I was about to go forward with the worst decision I had ever made. To others, I looked fine and gave no one any reason for concern, but I kept on hearing my mother's words: *Son, don't do it!* I should've called the wedding off well before that day, but I simply didn't have the courage. I knew I didn't mean it when I said, "I do". It took us only four months to destroy our relationship and five more to undo the marriage.

After the divorce, I was reassigned to a new unit overseas, and I decided to focus one hundred percent on being a soldier. My ordeal had left my total soldier performance a little lacking. I was accustomed to leading my peers in all areas of soldiering, but I allowed outside interests to have the most of my attention. I returned to living in the barracks, and for a time, that helped to reset the left and right borders of my soldierly life. It took about six months, but I managed to restore my discipline and performance standards back to respectable levels and began to hunt for career-enhancing opportunities.

THE AIR ASSAULT CHALLENGE

I learned that in the military, opportunities are yours to achieve not because of whom you know but because of your knowledge of and ability to match up with the criteria. In 1990, with my career being only three years old, I had aspirations to attend the assessment and selection program for special forces. At that time, I was assigned to an aviation unit in Panama. I watched the special ops soldiers do all sorts cool stuff including parachute jumps and rappelling from helicopters. I was just an aircraft door gunner and communications specialist who wanted to do more elite soldiering. I had done some pretty cool training up until that point, but I hadn't seen tactical training on that level before.

I found the Special Operations Battalion Command building and went in to speak to their command sergeant major (CSM) about how to transition to special forces, and he laid out a plan for me to transfer to his unit so I could undergo preparatory training that would prepare me at least physically for the assessment and selection program for special forces. When my first sergeant (1SG) heard about what I had done, he chewed me out a bit because my actions had not followed protocol, but he asked me what I really desired to do. I told him I wanted to do *Hooah!* stuff like the special ops soldiers. So he offered me an opportunity to compete for a chance to attend the Air Assault School, which would be held in Panama at the Jungle Warfare School that year. I immediately rogered up for it, but there was one problem; I had to outperform twenty other handpicked soldiers in a preselection competition to get one of only six available slots.

Our CSM chose the Army Physical Fitness Test (APFT) as the event to determine who would get the six slots. Twenty-six soldiers and NCOs were to compete for the six slots. The CSM chose the toughest grading scale to grade us all with equally because the Air Assault School (back then) was pretty grueling. A lot of units sent their finest soldiers to that school only to have them not make it through Day Zero and be sent back to their units that same day (we called it the duffle bag drag). But all I needed was the opportunity. I pitied the 1SGs of the other companies who put their best candidates up against me that day. My determination was so high that my 1SG could've given me Air Assault wings the moment I'd come out of his office with only a chance to compete. There was no way I would miss out on my chance to become Air Assault. I saw it as a step closer to becoming a Special Forces Green Beret.

My CSM also thought it would be good to add another degree of difficulty to the two-mile run of the test by choosing a route that hosted two quarter-mile hills. The standard APFT by army regulation called for a relatively flat surface like a running track, but since it was not an official test, he took some liberties. The slots would go to the six soldiers with the highest scores (300 being the highest you could score). I scored a 298 and still got only the fourth slot. That was the kind of competition I was up against. I was glad to have obtained the slot and personally gave my respect to the three who outperformed me and received the first three slots. I might have been in the top three had I not gotten a bug in my mouth during the last half-mile of the run. I had to swallow it without throwing up or breaking my stride, but that kind of slowed me down a bit. I was happy that I had gotten a slot, but I knew I still had to make it through the notorious Day Zero and the actual Air Assault School itself.

Day Zero was a day I'll never forget. When I finished, I was so tired that I didn't know if I had enough in my tank to start Day One of the school. But it was an unprecedented moment for me, as I became the only soldier out of my battalion's six candidates to make it through to Day One. Thanks to the type of physical and mental training I got during my first two years of service, I was well equipped to navigate all the challenges the Air Assault cadre threw at us. Make no mistake about it—it was tough, but it also resembled the normal physical fitness training conditions of my former infantry battalion.

On Day Zero, I watched so many soldiers do the duffle bag drag back to their units. I also listened to other candidates whine about their buddy getting sent back while a female soldier made it through Day Zero (as if she were the reason for their buddy's inability to persevere). They thought ignorant thoughts about her being there to fill some sort of quota or because the cadre liked her and didn't want to send her home. In my eyes, she was simply tougher and more capable than her critics realized. I witnessed it; they didn't cut her any slack, but they didn't have to; she was meeting all the expectations of the instructors while the other guys were busy trying to figure out how to game the obstacle courses and other physically demanding events.

With the Day Zero challenges increasing and everyone's energy decreasing, I drew determination from her as the day dragged on. And we drew strength from each other whenever we needed to as we became members of the same squad for the duration of the school. (Teamwork is forged in times like this.) For instance, when we got to the rappelling phase of the school, she met her match. She had a problem with heights, but I didn't. When it was our squad's turn to mount the fifty-foot tower, she looked at me, and I saw fear all over her face. I'd seen that look on the faces of some guys in my old platoon when we had to rappel down a high tower or mountainside for the first time. I addressed the matter with her privately while our turns were rapidly approaching. I asked her if she wanted to forfeit all that sweat and pain she had endured so far because of a fear of heights. She said no. I told her she needed to get that fearful look off her face before one of the cadre officers saw it. We both knew that that was not the type of attention you wanted from them. She said that someone in her unit hadn't paid attention while she was rappelling one time and she had been seriously injured.

I said, "Get behind me. I'll go first. I'll be your belay man on the ground, and I will *not* let you fall!" She agreed, and when it was her turn, she rappelled down the tower like a champ while other candidates continued to criticize her successes.

In previous qualifying ruck march events, we carried our weapons and the thirty-five-pound rucksacks we'd been carrying on our backs every day for the previous two weeks. On those, we were required to complete a four-mile ruck march in one hour and a six miler in ninety minutes. On the final qualifying ruck march, a twelve-miler in three hours, she left no doubt about her abilities. She was the third soldier over the line, and she did it in two hours and fifteen minutes. That commands the utmost respect from any soldier in any era. She passed me up on the trail as if I'd been standing still. She was sitting, laughing, and eating fruit by the time I came in fifteen minutes later. She was the only female to graduate from that Air Assault School, and I was more excited about her achievement than I was about mine.

My Air Assault School achievement and other successes put the spotlight on me with my chain of command, and a requisition came down from Major Command Headquarters for a soldier to be reassigned to the commanding general's drivers' team. Normally, when requisitions came down, unit commanders usually sent their most troubled soldiers so that they could be someone else's problem for a while. But in this case, a commander would choose a soldier who would best represent his unit as the soldier would be working in direct view of the four-star general in command over all the US forces in the region. I was selected for that duty for the next six months. I was taught how to drive tactically and placed in the rotation.

After completing the assignment, I had only six months left on my first enlistment, and I encountered circumstances that I hadn't foreseen. My plan upon reenlisting was to be reassigned to the special forces unit as I was invited to do by the Special Operations Command sergeant major and embark on the plan to eventually attend the Special Forces' Assessment and Selection program. Instead of being approached by the retention NCO, who was appointed to foster the army's retention of soldiers who were eligible for reenlistment, I was given orders for separation from the army.

In disbelief, I ignored the separation orders for about two months. When I reengaged the reenlistment issue, I found out that nothing I had achieved had been documented in my official military file, which meant that I was not eligible for reenlistment. My physical fitness test scores had stayed in the 290 to 300 range. It was normal for me to qualify expert with my rifle. I had retaken the military aptitude test and improved my scores in every category making me eligible for any opportunity the army had to offer. I had graduated from the Air Assault School making me only one of four air assault–qualified personnel in my battalion. I had been handpicked for the generals' drivers' team. I had also been awarded three impact awards given to those who perform something in a manner that exceeded expectations. If all that had been in my record of achievements, I would have been allowed to pursue my desire to move on to greater things as a professional at arms, a career soldier. Instead, my active-duty service was terminated in April 1993.

THE BACK-HOME NIGHTMARE

I returned to my hometown quietly heartbroken over my inability to reenlist and continue my career. I had no desire to be a civilian. (No disrespect to those whose liberty I knew I was defending.) I had done all that it took to be a soldier in the US Army. I had developed multiple skills as a soldier, and I had earned the credentials to operate very expensive equipment. I had flown on multimillion-dollar aircraft and was qualified on many different types of weaponry. I had even been on missions to other countries that I am not at liberty to speak about. But somehow, I found myself back home with my parents and siblings as if none of that had ever happened. I needed to figure out what to do with the rest of my life.

I really appreciated how my father dealt with me during that difficult time. We didn't speak about what had caused me to end up back home, but he knew I'd find a way to get back on my feet. Despite our silence, I knew my father saw how broken up I was about it and still had confidence in me; he wanted to support me. I was at a very low point in my life, and he knew I needed his confidence, not his pity.

Believing my military days were over, I pondered which way to go with my life. Being a career soldier was what I most desired, but I thought that chance had been taken from me. I couldn't think straight. My heart was infirmed in an indescribable way. I was about seventeen when I had seen a newly drafted NFL player suffer a career-ending injury on the first play of his first pre-season game. I think he must have felt the same way I was having been sent home by the organization I most desired to be a part of.

I couldn't let my dream of being a career army soldier go, so I signed up with the local army reserve, which was glad to have me. I thought that I could at least get my tactical training fix once a month. In the meantime, I knew I needed to man up, get a job, and move on with my life, so I went to the unemployment office for some assistance. The agent offered me unemployment benefits, but I turned them down. I told her that I was employable, that I just needed a job.

She asked me about the skills I had attained in the army, and I mentioned my weapons skills. She said that the office was receiving requests for security guards, and I said I was up for the challenge. I signed on with a firm that assigned me to a teachers' credit union. The pay was low, but I was back in a uniform and was again given the chance to serve the public; that helped me feel better about the job. I tried to save every cent until I could find employment that would sustain me at a decent quality of life.

As the weeks went on, it became clear that I could not continue to do the job for only $7 an hour. I needed a higher-paying job as soon as possible. I decided to resign and to tell my supervisor that coming Friday. But on the Tuesday prior to that, ten minutes into my routine lunch break, the bank manager frantically ran into the breakroom to tell me that the bank had just been robbed. I went back out to the bank floor to find that the two young men had already fled the bank with about $2,000. The manager called the police, and I called my supervisor. The teller said that one of the robbers had passed her a note stating that they would kill her if she didn't give them the money in her drawer. One of them insinuated that he had a pistol in the pocket he had his hand in. She had done as instructed.

When my supervisor arrived, the bank manager told him how disappointed she was with our company's services. I agreed with her assessment. During my first week on the job, I had told my supervisor that the bank was vulnerable whenever I took a break. I had suggested having two guards versus a lone star, but he had said the bank didn't want to pay for that and that the security firm didn't have enough personnel. I had often skipped lunch breaks when there were too many customers there, but when my supervisor found out about that, he instructed me to take my lunchbreaks. As a result of the unfortunate event, the security firm lost the account and I lost my job. I knew of no security guard who actually got robbed and fired for taking an authorized lunchbreak. The whole situation just added to my knowing that I was not where I should be.

Unable to find suitable employment, I took a job as a janitor. I was added to a team that cleaned a bank building downtown. The work was easy, but I was earning less than a thousand a month. I had one thought as I signed the employment agreement: *I was meant for much more than this!* I didn't want to live with my parents any longer, so I planned to save enough to cover six months' rent and utilities.

Day after day, I cleaned floors and took away the trash of those working in their chosen professions while thinking about having lost mine. My negative thinking made my job harder as the weeks dragged on. My desire to continue with my plan began to weaken as I would go home day after day and face my mother and father. They were supportive and didn't pry much, but just being in their presence became harder to bear; I felt that their expectations for me were much higher than what I was actually displaying.

My siblings and friends would ask, "When are you going back to the army?" or "Did the army kick you out?" or "Why can't you get back in?" Those questions tormented me long after they had been asked. I felt great rejection as I pondered how my life was turning out. To combat that, I stopped interacting with my friends. I made sure I was never where they frequented. I also stopped going home right after work; I would wait until I thought everyone was asleep and then go home. That practice evolved into my sleeping in my car until I knew the house would be empty the next morning. I would go home to clean up while everyone was at work or school. Not long after that, I made the complete transition to living out of my car.

GOTTA GET BACK IN

After weeks of living out of my car, I came to myself. I was shocked by the reality that I was living like a homeless person even though I didn't have to, and I knew I couldn't continue that style of living.

A few days later, I went over to my reserve unit to speak with my commander about preparations for an upcoming drill weekend. Somehow, we started discussing the turmoil I was feeling for not being able to pursue my army career on active duty. He said that my active-duty career didn't have to be over. He showed me in the army regulations that because of my honorable discharge, I was permitted to reenter the army with the same rank I had had at separation if I submitted my application for reentry within 180 days after my previous separation date. Four of those six months had passed, but the opportunity was still there. My reentry application required me to get consent to be released from the army reserves, and my reserve commander said he would gladly draw up the paperwork and sign it by the end of the week.

The previous four months had felt like years of aimless wandering. I had been losing hope fast. But that reserve officer breathed life back into my hope. The next morning, I was waiting for the army recruiters outside the recruiting station. I told them what I was there to do, and they were very unenthusiastic about it. I understood their position on my situation as I represented nothing but additional work for them; their responsibility was to add new recruits to the army, not help older ones reenter. Getting me back into the army would not count toward their monthly quota.

Being in the recruiting station among active-duty members gave me the first moment of comfort since my last days on active duty four months earlier. I was breathing army air and talking army lingo again. I spent most of the day there, and they treated me like I was a fellow service member again. It felt really good.

However, the next day, the commander of the recruiting station informed me that his recruiters didn't have the time to finish my reentry paperwork because they hadn't completed the paperwork for their new recruits. I offered to finish my paperwork for them if they would allow me to use their computers and check my work when I finished. He agreed, and I got the application packet done in two days.

I went to my parents' house to apologize and to speak to my father about where I'd been, what I'd been doing, and what my plans were. I asked him if I could return home to prepare for my final departure, and he agreed that that would be the best thing for me to do. It felt more as if he was going to suggest that I come home, but I simply asked first. Being back home allowed me to recover from the hard living I'd been doing.

Two weeks later, I was back in my army uniform. The nightmare that had been my life up until then was finally over. Being back in uniform and on an actual army installation was the real return home for me. Everything just snapped back into place. I had developed a little pudginess around my waistline and my physical fitness abilities were diminished, but I fixed that in no time.

CHAPTER 6

ROCK BOTTOM

REACHING ROCK BOTTOM

I'm sure some readers agree that anger can take them places and make them do things they end up regretting.[3] Being upset about how something didn't go well for you or being angry about how poorly your life is going in general can help you plot a course of destructive acts that can come with grave consequences.

I was that guy in 1994, just a year after returning to active duty. I was two years away from a critical point in my newly revived military career where I would have to be promoted soon or have to leave the army again; the army requires soldiers to be promoted at a certain pace if they wanted to remain on active duty. I still had two years, but I felt that time drawing near, and I was becoming overly concerned about it.

Instead of doing what would help me be promoted, I began to uncharacteristically get in trouble with my chain of command. I began to miss formations and receive what they called corrective actions for that. It seemed I'd be put out of the military rather than being retained. That had not been my plan. I didn't know how to fix it, and I didn't have anyone to mentor me on how to get it done. I kept on in the way I was going hoping I could get better at what I was expected to do and be, but I was becoming even more discouraged by witnessing younger soldiers with less time in service being promoted over me.

I now know that every person has his or her own rock bottom, and I was heading for mine though I didn't realize it. I thought I had reached my rock bottom once before. Reaching your rock bottom is what is called in certain circles giving up the ghost. It's that moment when you have counted the cost and determined that what you're doing is not worth the price you're paying for it. It's that moment that you sever your relationship with whatever is holding you back.

I imagine that the things I had been through would have been way past what many others could've endured. Yet, the depth of my rock bottom was still a little deeper though I didn't know that then.

When I came back on active duty, I began drinking again, but I acknowledged that alcohol was a problem for me, so I decided to drink only on weekends. I couldn't afford self-inflicted wounds that would hinder my quest to be the best soldier I could be. But before I knew it, I found myself drinking during the work week again and getting into altercations with people who outranked me. My drinking was also the reason for not hearing the alarm clock and missing first formations.

While racing toward my rock bottom, I received three Article 15s in fifteen months; those were stern warnings issued by my commander.

But more important, they were major showstoppers for my promotion. What was even more damaging was that they were all received while I was in the same unit, which was virtually unheard of at that time. In any other case, something more detrimental to one's career would have happened by the time your commander would consider administering a third Article 15. The two commanders that issued them had the same professional opinion: "I still see potential in you, soldier!"

I held my head up through them all, but I considered myself an embarrassment for the leaders before then who had invested in me becoming an army leader of the future. I was dubbed by prominent opinionates, "The worst soldier we got." I first took it as constructive criticism, but then I realized they really thought of me as the worst soldier in the unit. I couldn't disagree with that. I felt I was the only soldier in the unit doing wrong things at that time. As embarrassed as I was, I was determined to in army jargon fix myself. I refocused my mind and set out to improve my tactical, technical, and physical fitness performances, but I quickly realized that I had very little room for improvement and my problem was not in any of those areas.

However, I didn't know what to change. I needed a mentor, someone to tell me what I should be doing. I was nowhere near becoming an NCO than I was before all the troubles, and I still had no clue what to do about it. Most soldiers would've given up the dream by then. I watched many soldiers do just that and go home, but I couldn't. I knew I was supposed to be an NCO though I did not know what I would be doing in those upcoming years. Nor did I realize that once I became an NCO, I would be one for twenty-one years.

One day, I had a profound awakening to the root of all my problems. I discovered why I wasn't being recommended for promotion. The night before that fateful day, I had had a "few" beers. I set my alarm clock as I had always done. I don't remember much about that night, but I do remember the alarm clock waking me up. I yanked the power cord out of the wall and threw the clock across the room wondering why the alarm clock had gone off. I pulled the covers back over my head and went back to sleep.

An hour and a half later, I woke up in a panic realizing I had overslept. I had just missed our daily physical fitness training, which was also the unit commander's daily personnel accountability formation. We called it first formation or PT formation. I had been officially unaccounted for having missed that formation again. This formation is a very big deal for every unit commander.

The prescribed corrective action for my infraction was for me to report to the battalion's staff duty officer in different uniforms every two hours during off-duty hours for the next two weeks. Again, my hopes of being recommended for promotion were pushed back. The truth was staring me in the face. I regrettably had to learn that the hard way. Alcohol consumption was my problem. I didn't know how to fix it, and I was ashamed to tell anyone. Everyone I knew drank more than I did, and every event in the army professional or otherwise involved alcohol. So my grand solution was to abstain from alcohol altogether. That was quickly revealed to be a foolish idea as all my associations involved alcohol; it was almost impossible to not drink let alone keep it a secret that I had quit drinking. I felt that if it became common knowledge that I had stopped drinking, I would face criticism and more important be labeled an alcoholic, which would draw the attention of my chain of command. So that solution lasted only a few weeks.

With that going on, I could not keep an interest in having a relationship with anyone. I decided to remove myself from every association I had and simplify my life. That was all I knew to do at the time to fix myself.

Then a memory from years ago came roaring back, the memory of what was said and shown to me when I was young—the image of a wife and sons and the peace and joy that came with them. I didn't have any semblance of that peace or joy in my life then. I had had no relationships with females up to that time that gave me any hope of achieving it. I was so starved for success and ready for my life to have any kind of forward momentum that I got on my knees in that barracks room and prayed. "Lord, I need you to help me.[1] I'm losing everything. I'm tired of living like I'm living. I believe that you have a wife for me like you showed me while sitting on that porch as a kid. That's what I'm ready for. Please send her to me. I'll mess it up if I continue to search for her like I've been doing, so I'm not doing that anymore."

I stopped looking for her through relationships. I began to focus on getting back to becoming the best soldier I could be. Three weeks later, the two friends I had kept asked me to come over and hang out with them that night. I told them no. I felt that they would pull me back into the lifestyle I had just turned my back on. The next morning, they called me again asking me to come over. After their pleading with me, I agreed to go over. I took my time getting there and didn't put on any decent clothing. I wanted only to get them off my back and see what the fuss was all about.

When I stepped into the house, I saw what the fuss was all about. I walked into the long, galley-style kitchen, and at the other end were three young ladies. Two of them noticed me, and I acknowledged them by saying hello. But when the third young lady turned around and her eyes met mine, an explosion went off in me like I'd never felt before. I attempted to keep my cool while I tried to understand what was happening. It wasn't that she blinded me with her beauty. I had never seen her before and didn't know her name, but what happened next transformed everything in my life. As we looked into each other's eyes, I felt frozen in time. I heard, *That's your wife!*

She looked at me as if she was having her own revelation. She turned around to continue what she had been doing as if nothing had just happened. I knew that I had heard the truth, but all I could do was walk out of the room. I knew that I had just seen the woman I'd been looking for for the past eighteen years, and later, I found that her name was Monique. I told myself, *Man! I got to get my act together!* It took me six months to do that.

Nearly every decision I made from then on had adding her to my life as my overall objective. I never allowed anyone to know what had happened or what was in my heart or my thoughts. I simply attended to my affairs for the purpose of receiving her into my life. Once I began, I realized I had everything to fix. Everything in my life needed my attention. Only the aspects of my life directly related to soldiering were in good shape. My finances were a wreck, and even my car needed major work.

As I set about squaring my business away, I was internally embarrassed about how neglected my personal affairs were. I became thankful that I had had to wait for her because it gave me the time to present myself a little better. Before I took a hard look at my affairs, I thought I had reached my rock bottom and maybe I was on my way up out of my mess. However, without truly finding a solution to my drinking problem, I finally hit my true rock bottom about four months after meeting Monique. It took an incident just as grave as the life-changing event in my car a few years earlier to do that. That night, I knew I had finally hit bedrock.

THE ACTUAL BOTTOM

About four months after I had had the privilege of meeting my wife-to-be, I was still trying to get my affairs in order. Things were finally going well for me as a soldier. The clouds hovering over my career were beginning to break. Even the leaders who knew about my mishaps began to transfer out, and I received a new immediate supervisor who seemingly cared about my career progression. Things were finally beginning to swing my way.

Then it happened. Monique invited me to her university's homecoming football game that coming Saturday. Excited about where that could lead, I told her I would be there. I had been waiting for the opportunity (that I knew would eventually come) to spend time with her. I thought this could be that time. Everything was finally lining up. I was bursting with anticipation. I tried to patiently wait for Saturday, but I had nothing to do the night before, and I had already done everything I could to prepare for the big day.

I was so bored and restless Friday night. Most young soldiers like me lived for what we called payday weekends; the weekends when we had the most fun. A payday just happened to fall on the Friday of her university's homecoming weekend. I simply needed to wait patiently for the next day to start my payday festivities. I had never had to sit out a Friday night before. That was asking a lot for a young soldier with a pocketful of money, and I just couldn't do it. I had no plans to go out that evening, but I made some. I figured I would go to the club for a little while and get back to the barracks early—like midnight. But by the time I picked up a friend and made it there, I was in my regular game mode as though it were a typical weekend.

Within an hour at the club, I found myself in a disagreement with someone I didn't know. I didn't think much of it until I realized he was not going to let it go. I knew I was in trouble. I told my friend that it was time to go, and we made it over to one of the club security officers, who told us to leave. I believed he held the guy and his three friends up in the club to give us a chance to drive off, but I delayed leaving. I was enraged at the thought of walking away from a fight; that went against everything I'd been taught growing up. By what we called street code, you would eventually have to face that person before the disagreement could ever be truly resolved. A wiser person would've left and lived to fight on better terms. The odds were not in favor of my coming out of that engagement unscathed. But I'd had a few drinks in the club, and the alcohol had begun to take effect. A sense of boldness—actually, foolish thinking—came over me as I watched those guys come out into the parking lot.

I found myself in a physical altercation with the four guys. In the first few seconds of the fight, I received a blow to my temple that rang my bell. One guy hit me with a snub-nosed, six-shot revolver. As I dashed between two parked cars I heard him fire six shots. I was astonished that he had not hit me at that short range. Figuring he had to reload at that point, I ran through a frantic group of people for about fifty yards into some woods and lay down in the dirt and brush. As I lay there, I thought I should have had gunshot wounds in my back or head and fighting to stay alive but had escaped. Even an inexperienced shooter with eyes closed could've gotten me with at least one shot being as close to the shooter as I was. I believed that the same angel that had saved me from being killed by the speeding car when I was five and had saved me from killing myself while driving under the influence of alcohol four years earlier. This night he had shielded me from the bullets.

I started to think that the shooter might have missed me on

purpose and was only trying to scare me, but then I saw him entering the woods and reloading. It was clear to me that he intended to finish me off and had not missed on purpose. Lying on the ground and bleeding from my head, I thought, *I'm too old for this!* I decided that if I got out alive, I'd not put myself in these kinds of situations ever again. I had officially reached rock bottom.

The shooter finally gave up the search for me and I eventually got back to my barracks. My car was still in the club parking lot and I had no idea what had happened to the friend who had gone to the club with me. In that moment of silence I reflected on the havoc I had created for myself and others in just a couple of hours.

I woke up on homecoming date day with my pillow covered in blood, and my head swollen on one side. There was no way I could meet her in that condition. Too embarrassed to face her, I simply stood her up. It took me two weeks to get up the courage to call and tell her what had happened; that gave time for the swelling to go down in case she wanted to see me. She didn't appreciate being stood up, but she graciously understood and forgave me. A few more weeks passed before I finally saw her again.

I recovered from the incident and miraculously retained her interest, but I still didn't have it all together. Even though we got together, I still had a major problem that was controlling some things in my life—alcohol. It had nearly cost me my life more than once. It was threatening my career and could cause me to lose my relationship with the one I'd been looking for all my life. And that scared me. My response to that of course was to grab something to drink.

Alcohol had caused me many major problems, and I knew I needed to get free of it. Finally, I got strength enough to completely walk away from it all. And it came from a most unlikely source: Monique. We had been together for about a month when she told me, "Baby, I don't like you drinking." That was all I needed to break free. I guess I just needed someone to care enough about me to take a stance against it and say something.

Up to that point, I'd simply been doing what everyone else

had been doing. No one around me ever did anything that didn't involve alcohol; that was the culture among soldiers back then. You were expected to hold your liquor to make sure you never have any documentable alcohol-related incidents. Monique got no fight from me. I told her okay. I poured all my liquor down the drain as she watched, and it took me a while because I had so many bottles, another embarrassing moment.

Every moment she and I spent together was quality time; we learned about one another and shared with each other. When she moved in with me, we took long walks in the evening and talked for hours. Experiencing her rewired how I thought about everything. We realized that life would be better if we lived it together. We married thirteen months later.

With alcohol out of the picture, I was able to think clearly and focus on my career and my future with her. She was the catalyst that made me redefine my relationship with everything in my life. In my heart and mind, many new things gained prominence while others I'd thought were important began to lose value or be removed from my life.

As I restructured my life, opportunities came to me. The pressure to stay in the army had been mounting and being married brought the added pressure of having to provide us financial stability. We agreed early on not to have children until we had financial stability to an acceptable degree. Those pressures were lifted once I was promoted to sergeant. Then less than a year and a half later, I was promoted to staff sergeant.

CHAPTER 7

OUR CHALLENGES BEGIN

Before my promotion to staff sergeant, I was sent on an unaccompanied tour overseas for a year. That was the first time Monique and I were apart from one another. We did not realize how great of a challenge it would be, and we were not prepared for it. We had to figure out how to live apart, and my additional military entitlements were cut off the month after I arrived at my new assignment overseas; that made it extremely difficult to pay our mortgage and other things.

We had been trying to have a child for the better part of two years, but Monique kept having miscarriages. After the last miscarriage, we were told that we weren't going to be able to have children, that if we wanted children, we should consider adoption. I was enraged that these things were being said not to me but to my wife, who was understandably vulnerable. What I was hearing was contrary to what had been shown me years before in that vision. Monique's being in my life was evidence that the entire vision would come true. Every word that was spoken to her pierced her heart, as I watched her emotional descent.

My father's challenges and victories came rushing back to me. I remembered when he had said that the doctor told him his daughter was dead and yet to their amazement, she was brought to life without their help. I remembered how I held in my arms the living evidence of my father's testimony eighteen days later. I refused to allow anyone to speak discouraging words into our lives. I interrupted the doctor knowing I was right about what I was going to say: "She will conceive, and we will have our own children!"

A little more than a year later, we were delivering our first child. My son was born premature at seven months, but he was well. His birth represented another level of faith and trust in God and further confirmed what He had shown me about my future. A man told me no, but God had already said otherwise. What He had shown me so many years before was manifest.

At the time of his birth, I was on the unaccompanied tour with nine months still remaining on the twelve-month assignment. I had spoken to my wife on the phone as we did every day I was away, and two hours after we had spoken, my chain of command notified me that I had a new boy. I was instantly set back knowing he was two months early. I had planned to take midtour leave around his birth date so I would be there for it.

Then they said Monique had had complications and had to be rushed to the hospital. She had had complications throughout the pregnancy. Most of her first trimester was spent in bed. We had done everything the doctors had suggested and everything we could find in books to make sure she and the baby made it through the first trimester, but nothing prepared us for the problems that surfaced right after he was born.

We were both quite excited when we found out that she was pregnant again. I knew that this was the time. However, she pinned all her enthusiasm on making it through the first trimester. Going into the third and fourth months, her belly began to grow and so did her excitement. All I did was love on her and do everything she wanted me to (which included me taking her to the store for her favorite thing then—watermelon). I was such a pushover, but she didn't take advantage of me. I didn't care what anyone thought about it either.

Very few in or around her and me knew what we were going through. We were very much joined at the hip in just about every matter, but then there we were literally half a world apart. The only thing I could do was call her every day to keep her encouraged.

I wasn't there when she went into her fifth month of pregnancy. She had a few friends there, but she didn't have me. I couldn't help with anything on the home front. My wife was left to do everything for all of us while she still had four more pregnancy months to go.

By the second month I was gone, the physical and financial frustrations of maintaining the house began to loom larger than ever for her. She had to figure-out how to purchase baby stuff, make sure the grass was cut, eat for two people, run around town and pay bills in person because internet banking was not as robust as it is today. She had to shop, do laundry, and even send me money to live on each month all because I wasn't there. On top of all that, be an active-duty soldier for the US Army. Although she was a real trouper, her stress level was very high, which made me believe that was why our son was born premature and only three pounds four ounces.

We had financial issues maintaining two households, and I still had nine months on my overseas tour to go. I took my midtour leave two months earlier than originally planned; I was expected back in thirty days, but I didn't think that would be enough time. My son would be in an incubator until he reached five pounds. Then he would still be on a unique liquid diet and have frequent medical appointments until he showed that he had no complications. Adding all that up basically said that this would take longer than thirty days.

I received what were called compassionate reassignment orders, which would have allowed me to be reassigned to a unit near my family. I was receiving a subsidy that helped cover a portion of my apartment lease overseas, but if I were reassigned back to the States, I believed I would have to repay $200 for each remaining month of my lease, and $200 then was too much for us to handle, so I decided to return to finish my overseas assignment. One of the dumbest decisions I ever made. Monique would have a baby to care for on top of everything else she was handling. This was all because I was too afraid of upsetting our financial situation any further. She agreed to it and trusted that I knew what was best for us as a military family, but it still put an obscene amount of pressure on her as a new mother. The truth was that I really didn't know what was best for us at that time. I didn't want to add any more financial stress to my family, but not being there to share in the daily responsibilities created more issues between my wife and me than I had ever imagined.

After I left, these unforeseen issues began to manifest themselves in the form of resentment, a single-mother complex, and feelings of abandonment. I was no help at all. I did find a way to generate more income to help with our finances, but that didn't ease the stress on my wife's everyday life. That's where the frustration was, not so much the money. Once I finally caught on to that, it was too late. The decision was made, and we had to endure it until the end. I thought we would somehow survive it because of our love for one another, but once we began to disagree and argue over the phone (for the first time ever), I realized that these next few months would challenge our marriage like nothing we had ever experienced.

Our relations had gotten to the point that it was difficult for us to have conversations without disagreeing on something. And within six months after I returned home, our relationship had deteriorated to the point that I was sleeping in the guest bedroom and the idea of getting a divorce was gaining ground.

After about three to four weeks of not really talking to each other, I finally put a stop to the whole thing. Standing in the dining room, I got my wife's attention as she came in the front door. She came over to me, and once I knew that she would receive my words, I said, "Look, I love you, and you love me! I'm not going anywhere, and you're not going anywhere! So we're gonna figure this out together, okay?" She said okay. I wasn't exactly sure how we were going to overcome our issues, but we were determined to figure it out together, not apart.

Military families constantly face challenges that are quite uncommon to civilian families. Every military member is engulfed in the endeavors of having a military career, which affects everyone in the family. It is a life not easily lived by any member of the household. We were two service members who created a family.

THE BIG MIRACLE

I returned home from the overseas assignment tour to be assigned to another hard-charging (heavily trained) unit. A year and a half had passed after my return, and even though half of it was spent on a four-month deployment to the Middle East and several training exercises out of state, Monique and I still managed to recover some from the troubles. But in the middle of our progress, my unit was selected to deploy to Europe in support of conflict resolutions there. We were notified by our commander that the task force would be assembled to depart within three or four months. At that moment, he might as well have said we were departing next week. All I could imagine was the door of hope for my marriage being slammed in my face. At that point, our relationship was still quite fragile, and in my experience, I believed it to be nearly impossible to build or rebuild a relationship while apart. Building a relationship requires close-quarter interaction.

The deployment was to be as long as nine to twelve months. Monique and I weren't out of the woods yet, and I wasn't sure if our marriage could withstand being apart for that long again only months after I had returned from a previous short-notice, four-month deployment overseas, which destroyed our plans for a family vacation. I thought the ultimate expectation of a soldier was to do their job while deployed, but I was also a husband, father, provider, and protector, but my soldierly duty and responsibilities as an NCO were to my fellow warfighters and the upcoming mission. I was greatly conflicted because I desired to be a family man and a soldier, but I couldn't figure out which was top priority and how to get it all done.

Two months went by. We had already sent our unit's equipment forward. We began to conduct all the necessary briefings and handle medical and dental matters, and all the other deployment protocols. In the midst of all that, I was inundated with rambling thoughts of how to keep my family together and my career intact. The military oath I took demanded that I fulfill the so-called higher purpose. While I interpreted the oath of enlistment in that way, it still did not sit well with me in my heart.

As I looked at everything that had transpired and everything we had been through to bring my wife and me to where we were at that moment, I was convinced that the whole scenario was wrong. I was committed to my marriage vows and the oath I took when I enlisted (including the NCO's creed), but I couldn't figure out how to merge them all into one state of being. I wanted to give a hundred percent to it all. During the 1990s, as I grew into being a young military leader, I watched divorce become the most prominent administrative action among military soldiers officers and enlisted alike, and it looked that we were headed toward adding to that growing statistic.

One could look at the condition of the armed forces back then and wonder why any soldier would ever consider getting married while on active duty. In 1995, I was doing exactly what I knew I should do with my life. I had also married the woman I loved, and I knew that I was right in doing so. I loved my family and could not believe that we had considered divorce. We had not agreed to go through all we went through to start a family just for me to become a military dad who only paid child support. These were the thoughts that plagued my mind during those last few weeks leading up to the deployment.

I was out of answers and thought I had nowhere to turn. So instead of calling my father, I called my mom (I would usually speak to my mom about matters of the heart). As I explained the situation to her, I became outwardly emotional about it for the first time. I didn't have much time to have a long, drawn-out discussion about it with her as I was nearing the end of my lunch break when I called. After I poured the whole issue out into her ear, all I got in response from her was, "Well, seems like you need to pray about that, son!" *I thought, Has it come to that? Maybe she doesn't have any wisdom for me on this issue.* For a second, I thought calling her had been a waste of time and considered getting upset with her for her words. But I took a pause. After I got off the phone with her, her words kept reverberating in my mind. I thought, *Well, I've tried everything except prayer.*

The only thing that offered me any hope at that moment was prayer. I remembered that all I was desperate to keep had happened because I had prayed. I remembered that God was the one who had given me a wife and a child. A notion came to my mind that if He had given them to me, then He could fix all this mess if I got on my knees and called on Him. Being so fed up with everything and being out of options, I got straight to the point: "God, if you're real, I got a real problem. My marriage is in trouble. My unit is deploying again in three weeks. If I deploy with them, my marriage is surely over. I want to keep my family and my career, and I want us to be a family again. You gave me that woman and saved my son's life. Surely you didn't give them to me just for me to lose them. If you can do anything to keep us together, I'm yours forever."[1] I got up and left the whole issue right there.

That following week, I received an official notification from the Department of the Army for a permanent transfer to a three-year special assignment with a nondeployable unit. It was an accompanied tour, which meant my wife and son could come along. I was in disbelief since my unit's deployment personnel roster had been solidified and sent up the chain to the division commander, a two-star general, for approval. I didn't believe that the special assignment orders would be strong enough to keep me from deploying with my unit even though they were official orders from the Department of the Army. When my immediate chain of command found out about the assignment orders, they basically dismissed it the way I initially had. For the moment, I chalked it up as simply a delight to the imagination. It finally dawned on me that that could possibly be our way out. I went to our battalion's administration office to request a hardcopy of the orders. Once I thoroughly read the orders, I realized that a miracle was happening. I felt compelled to make it a reality; I began to execute the standard out-processing procedures.

I called the senior NCO, the command sergeant major of the special unit to inquire about the new assignment, and he explained what the assignment was all about and that the search to fill the position had led to me, the only NCO with the correct credentials essential to the position available. This was not a coincidence; this was God's doing I was sure. No army leader would have such an interest in removing a key, essential leader from a unit two weeks prior to its deploying to a combat zone (though it was labeled as a training exercise). Labeling the deployment a training exercise kept every deploying soldier in that unit eligible for reassignment at any time.

When I looked back, I saw how God had strategically planned our escape from that situation years prior to that moment by giving me opportunities to obtain certain credentials that distinguished me from my peers at that unforeseen time of trouble. He then created a timely need for the use of those credentials that only I could fill at that particular moment. I also learned how the army regulations concerning special assignments (at that time) stated that the orders could not be undone at the division command level. This meant that the division commander, the two-star general, was unable to revoke the orders. I was instantly encouraged and relieved knowing that I had been chosen for the assignment and that no one had the authority to undo it.

I was finally called in by my chain of command to discuss the assignment orders. My commander and first sergeant asked me to personally request the cancellation of my new orders, but I declined to do that. I knew that transferring was the right decision, but I was still enticed by the opportunity to deploy with my unit, and I relished being a soldier in that capacity. I knew in my heart that I was born to be a soldier/leader. I enjoyed having the weight of responsibility on my shoulders as an NCO. I loved accomplishing tasks and missions as other soldiers followed my lead. Back then, before 9/11, the most alluring opportunity for an NCO was to be deployed to a combat-zone, lead soldiers, and not lose a single one. That was the surest way to a promotion. I knew that if I got promoted to the next rank, I'd get a substantial pay raise that would help me get my family out of debt, and I could then provide for them much better.

Having all those enticing thoughts going through my mind while standing before my chain of command, it reminded me that being overly ambitious was the catalyst for most military families being destroyed. I quickly came to the no-brainer understanding that there would be no family to speak of if I chose to forgo the special assignment and deploy with my unit, so I elected to keep the new assignment.

My decision did not go over very well with other NCOs of the unit. I had chosen my family over the mission, them and my career, and God used my career to answer my prayer, which gave me the ability to keep them both intact. With my turning the whole issue over to Him, He gave me the means to have my cake and eat it too, and we were in a better position to mend our relationship and grow stronger than we had ever been before.

CHAPTER 8

PROMOTION: GOD'S WAY

MY FATHER

Being promoted in the army as a young soldier through the first three ranks had come easy to me. I only had to be the young man my father had raised me to be. As a boy, I often had great disdain for the disciplines my father impressed upon me. I had no clue as to what it was all about. I thought he was simply trying to keep me from having fun. During the first week of my arrival to my basic training unit, drill sergeants who expected the new recruits' performances to be poor were initially astonished at how easily I comprehended and executed instructions. Putting my socks and clothes in drawers, cleaning my shoes after wearing them for training and storing them in a designated place and in an orderly manner while hanging my clothes in a closet in an organized manner had become second nature to me from age twelve on thanks to my father, who called it, "Clean up your room."

After I displayed my aptitude for handling basic training requirements, I was routinely called upon by my drill sergeants as an example to bring other soldiers' performances up to the basic training standard. While I was in basic, instead of my sergeants repeatedly explaining their expectations, they would simply send other privates to me for instruction. The drill sergeants stopped inspecting my area after the first week of training. Basic training was not the grueling, excessively challenging experience I thought it would be thanks to my father.

For whatever reason, my father raised me differently. His expectations of me were much higher than his expectations for my brothers and sisters, older and younger. He reared me to professional levels of soldiering. His tutelage embodied the core values of integrity, discipline, excellence, ownership, respect, courage, diligence, commitment, selfless service, confidence, balance, and loyalty. Of course, as a boy, I didn't have any understanding of what he was instilling in me. I was just trying to get things done so I could go outside and hang out with my friends. But as an adult, I can look back and easily conjure up instances where each one of these values became a focal point in my upbringing. By the time I left home, these values were engraved upon my heart though I didn't realize that.

As I matured, these values governed all I did and became the outward projection of my character. Did Pops know my destiny was to become a senior leader in the US Army? I don't know. What I do know is that his rearing of me made soldiering very basic. I thank God for my father.

One Sunday afternoon when I was seven, he and I were watching old war movies when I told him I was going to be a soldier when I grow up. Although he acknowledged my statement, his countenance lacked enthusiasm. Yet during my teenage years, he was the right stuff for me. At times, his unrelenting ways were challenging. I would sometimes hear my mother quietly pleading on my behalf. She would try to convince him to allow me to go and play before the day ended even though I hadn't completed my chores to the standard he expected. In some cases, I forfeited a day of play due to uncompleted chores or having done them poorly. If things were not done according to his expectations, they were simply done over. My father had standards by which I was to execute my chores. If I didn't meet his standards, I wasn't going anywhere. He was the only one allowed to declare something complete as he was the only inspector of all chores. His inspecting techniques aggravated me to no end. With my friends waiting on me to show up at the park to play football or basketball, I was sometimes delayed because of the do-overs of various chores.

I didn't have a problem with having chores. I simply disliked having to do them on Saturdays. As an active teenager, I really didn't have any other opportune time due to my weekdays being full of school, sports practice, homework, and my part-time job. A regular Saturday of chores included doing the laundry start to finish, cleaning the bathroom, picking up trash around the yard, plus mowing and raking the lawn, and that could take me until two in the afternoon.

One Friday night, I realized that if I got up earlier instead of sleeping in, I could get my chores done by ten or perhaps eleven allowing for some do-overs. He didn't tell me when to start, only when I was finished. My determination woke me up that morning instead of the alarm clock, and I went straight to work. I was so determined to make the plan work that I was done by nine.

Concerned about do-overs, I spent an additional hour checking my work based on my father's standards. I felt that my father was in my head looking through my eyes and pointing out every deficiency as I discovered them. Once I was confident that there weren't any shortcomings, I reported to my dad, who would be on the couch at that time of the day. At ten, the earliest I had ever reported to him, I proudly reported that I had completed all my chores. My father was not one to allow you to see him not calm, cool, and collected, but when he heard my report, just for a brief moment, I saw amazement come over his face. *Yeah, that's right!* I thought.

I waited for "Did you do this?" and "Did you do that?" and his getting up and doing his typical inspection of everything. That day, I was overconfident and prepared to gloat when he found nothing wrong or out of place. But that day of all days, he didn't do as I had anticipated. He simply said, "Well, good. So what are you going to do now? Are you going to the park to play ball?" I wasn't prepared for that response. He had never engaged with me in that fashion when it came to chores. He set me back on my heels a bit. I told him I was going to play basketball. He said, "Okay. Have fun. See you when you get back."

I didn't know whether to be glad or mad. All the way to the park, I tried to figure out what had happened. I was fully prepared to take the spoils of victory when suddenly he allowed me to go without being inspected. For my victory to be had, I felt I needed him to inspect my work and find nothing to poke at. That was how I defined success that morning, but I didn't get the proper responses for that to happen. I began to be upset at the thought that maybe he had intentionally forfeited just before I could claim victory. Then I thought about the many times in my life where it seemed as though he knew everything I was thinking or doing. Did he perhaps know my plan that morning, or could it be that that was the elevated performance he was looking for out of me all along?

We never spoke about it, but I sincerely believed (knowing my father's ways) that it was his intent to drive me toward taking ownership of the responsibilities that he had given me instead of him being the only person ensuring that things got done around the house. He was trying to get me to step up.

From that day forward, he never again inspected my chores or asked me if something was done or not. I took the reins that day. From then on, I decided when and how well things got done (based on my father's expectations of course). I even assumed responsibility for the chores of my younger brothers and sisters (what few they had). If they didn't do something well, I showed them how and made sure their jobs were done right. That's what my father was after; I'm sure of it.

He was a marine of the 1950s. He said that the army was soft compared to the Marine Corps then and now. So you can imagine the reaction I got when I told him I was joining the army. Not very many things got my father off his couch or the TV remote out of his hand when he was relaxing, but that announcement created a monumental moment. I was announcing this to a man whose service in uniform had ended almost thirty years prior, but he would still get off the couch to render a proper salute when the Marine Corps commercials came on, which I thought were the best commercials in the 1980s. However, I did not get that same patriotic response to my announcement. He jumped up off his couch and said, "What? If you're going to join any branch of service, it should be the Marine Corps like a real man." That exchange didn't go very well. His nurturing of me, however, was the foundation my military career was built upon for the better part of a thirty-year career.

PROMOTION TO SERGEANT
FIRST CLASS GOD'S WAY

It took me six years to be promoted from staff sergeant to sergeant first class. I discovered that as a Christian, I needed to trust God and do things His way to break through to the top three enlisted ranks in the army because my prospects for being promoted looked hopeless. I had done so much out of my own wisdom that I didn't know what else to do. After getting overlooked for the fourth year in a row, I thought I was done. I thought I should've been a no-brainer selectee that fourth year. Every senior leader who reviewed my records stated how they couldn't understand why I hadn't been promoted before then. Some said that some of my less-qualified peers had been promoted. I felt there was nothing else I could do.

Some of my peers who were selected that year offered me their condolences, assistance, and advice; I simply congratulated them and treated them with love and appreciation and moved on. The day the selection list was released, I went home embarrassed and told my wife that I hadn't been selected again. Then I went into my private place to get alone with God in prayer. I realized that I had been carrying my desire for promotion like a backpack that got heavier and heavier each year.[1] I decided that I wasn't going to carry it anymore. In prayer, I turned my promotion desires over to the Lord.[2] I put it down and did not pick it up again. I said, "Lord, I'm not carrying this anymore. I'm giving it to you, Father. If you want me to be promoted, then you do it. I'm done with it." I felt a load lift off my mind.

I couldn't understand why it seemed that God was in favor of my being promoted when it hadn't happened. It was as though God had a strategic plan for me that I didn't know about. But I continued to receive God's favor in the form of opportunities to attend military schools. With every opportunity, I felt peace and an unction to receive it and honor God with it. Some were a matter of the Father giving back to me the opportunities that had been lost or stolen in the past. Other opportunities were new initiatives based upon the Department of Defense's approach to winning the war on terrorism. Graduating from these schools built the case even stronger for my promotion to sergeant first class, but I didn't understand what the Lord was ultimately doing with me.

Not long after that year's selection list came out, I went on a fast. I questioned what my purpose really was in the military as a man of God, a Christian, and why my career was seemingly stagnant. I knew I needed to position myself so I would have no issues hearing the Lord. I needed answers! Well, by the third day of that fast, I got my answers along with instructions for moving forward.

THE VISION OF GOD'S ANSWER

During my fast, I was looking for understanding of why I should stay in the army. Once before, I had contemplated leaving the army, but the Lord had dealt with me swiftly concerning that. I knew I was to remain in the army. A few years later, 9/11 happened. Even if I had left the army then, I would've ended up raising my right hand again on 9/12.

I knew I was born and built for this generation's wars. On the third day of the fast, while I was giving God thanks, He gave me a vision of young men along a red clay road buried up to their necks. As I walked down the road, each person raised his hand as if to beg me to help pull them out of the clay dirt, which in the heat hardens almost like concrete. I grabbed the first person's hand and pulled him out. It took all of our combined strength for him to break free. I began to brush the clay off him and his clothing. I helped the next and then the next young man in the same manner, and the message became clear—God wanted me there to help others who were oppressed, depressed, or otherwise held back and help develop them into men of honor who could realize their destinies and move into them.

Why a Christian in the army? That's why. I considered the armed forces a mecca for young men and women trying to figure out what their purposes in life were. In most cases, the love of God would draw them to me, or I would find myself directly involved with their issues. Without even my prying, they would open up to me about what they were going through. I never took those moments for granted. I realized that my purpose was to be the vessel through which God could get in on their lives and help. I now understood that He called for me to be His man in the army. By the time the Lord showed me that vision in prayer, I had been operating in that capacity for Him for years. My heart had long since been tenderized for such a calling. God designed me to have a real compassion for people. I took every opportunity to help those who were on a trajectory to intersect with me as the Lord led me of course all the way to the point of my literally giving the shirt off my back at times.

My wife and I had always prayed for insight and understanding when I received new assignment orders. I called God my career manager. I allowed Him to decide for me and the army where He needed me to be. As I consider my decades of service and the medals and stripes I earned, I am in awe of what God did with my career after I put it in His hands. Everywhere I went, whatever unit God assigned me to, I was the right stuff for His purpose there. And because He assigned me to my units, I fit well with the chains of command and was never a disappointment to them or the army.

The places and positions the Lord assigned me to were nothing short of great exploits. From the East to the West Coasts and from below the equator to the northernmost parts of the continental United States plus at least eight other countries, God gainfully employed me with His purposes in mind. My most constant thought was to never discount where I'd been sent.

Purpose exists for us all. To not seek out and find what your purpose is can cause you to miss out on your destiny's call in that place and moment of your life. You can also miss out on the benefits of your purpose. It is very possible for some to walk blindly through their lives and miss just about everything God has for them.

Having experienced some lifesaving events, I vowed to maintain a macro vision approach to everything I am and everything I do everywhere I am sent. I had been blessed with the privilege of continuing to live, and I refused to walk through life like an automaton with no regard for others or for my purpose.

I still have a purpose or I wouldn't still be here, and that purpose benefits me and others. Many things about me are yet to be revealed, but thank God, my future purposes will be unveiled as I continue to walk it out. Receiving that vision from God answered the most pressing question of my heart and confirmed that I was not to leave the military. I was a noncommissioned officer because that was His will for me.

More than anything, I wanted to do His will as a military leader, and I was reinvigorated to do so despite not being promoted that year. Promotion took the back seat in my heart that day. I continued to study His Word, and I came to understand that promotion is God's will for our lives.[3] Psalm 75:6 tells us, "Promotion cometh neither from the east, nor from the west, nor from the south. But God is the judge: He putteth down one, and setteth up another."

My problem was that I had put being promoted higher on my priority list than it should've been. I turned my career over to God though I didn't know what He would do with it, but I knew He wanted me to remain in the army. I realized that I could not retire as a staff sergeant and that He would have to promote me to sergeant first class if He wanted me to continue doing His will in the military. I also questioned how He would do it. Up to then, I had been denied promotion so many times that I thought something in my records I didn't know about was disqualifying me.

As I continued in my study time and prayer life, I was reminded of how big God really is. I acknowledged in my heart that I had placed God in a position inferior to that of the promotion selection board members. Somehow, I had it in my mind that people had the power to override God's judgment concerning what happened to me. So all my efforts up till that point were done to appease the promotion selection board members. Every year that I put myself at the mercy of people instead of under the authority of God, I was denied promotion. "No more!" I declared. I realized He could turn the heart of any person[4] as is stated in Proverbs 21:1: "The king's heart is in the hand of the Lord, as the rivers of water; He turneth it withersoever he will." I reminded myself that God was superior to people, not the other way around. The creature is not above its creator! I repented and repositioned myself under His authority and was promoted to sergeant first class the next year. It was that simple!

PROMOTION TO MASTER SERGEANT

It was not long after that promotion that I became eligible for promotion to master sergeant. As uncanny as it was, I spent only two and a half years as a sergeant first class before I was updating my records again for the upcoming promotion board. I reviewed the criteria for promotion and realized that I met them all; I was a top-tier candidate, but being looked at in the secondary zone (that is, the group that is eligible for the first time). However, I still prayed and asked Him what He would have me do. The Lord asked me, *What is your special missions unit's key initiatives?* I told Him that it was to provide the regular army task forces with solutions to the asymmetric threats in any combat theater. He asked, *What do you think is lacking in all that?* I said that the task force's missions were not supported logistically as well as they could be. In a lot of cases, the execution phase of even the smallest tactical mission could easily turn into a disaster of sorts if not properly supported.

I thought that the logistical arm of the task forces could be deployed in a more-informed way that would produce a much more robust posture for logistical support before, during, and after every mission. He asked, *What are you going to do about that?* I realized what He was doing. I was asking him what I should do to be promoted, but He was asking me questions that had nothing to do with being promoted. I knew His ways enough to know that that meant I should no longer concern myself with how He was going to promote me; rather, I should focus on what He had put me in that unit to do. Basically, He was telling me, *Do your job and I'll do mine!* I let my concern for promotion go and kept with God's train of thought. I told Him, "I need to know how to better equip the task force's support teams and bridge the gap between them and the additional unknown avenues of support available to them in their combatant commander's area of responsibility that would enable task force commanders to improve the success rate of their missions."

By that time in my career, I had deployed enough times and had leveraged these entities that existed across the army's echelons and other branches of service as well as other coalition forces in Iraq and Afghanistan. I began to devise a step-by-step chart that would show the regular army task force support teams how to tap in to those resources.

The Lord reminded me of the Army Logistics University, so I read its course catalog, and the Lord unctioned me to pursue four courses that would help me bridge the gap: joint logistics, multinational logistics, performance work statements, and the combat capabilities development course. I thought I would get some pushback for requesting to attend these courses, which would take two months, but then I realized that the Lord had pointed me to those courses and therefore favor would be applied to my requests.

I created a PowerPoint presentation to highlight the issue to my chain of command and show how I could train task force logisticians to leverage every source of logistical support available in their areas of operation. My presentation was a hit. They were aware of the problem, but up until that moment, they hadn't had enough personnel to target the issue. At that time, I was only the 198th soldier to go through the assessment and selection process and be accepted into the new special missions unit.

There I was hitting one of the nails on the head for the Pentagon's Army Staff. God had done it again; He had impressed something on my heart and positioned me to be a problem solver for the army. My commander gave me permission and a blank check to pursue any schooling I deemed necessary to fulfill my plan. I felt it prudent to get my peers involved so I wouldn't be the only subject-matter expert. I knew that together we could get the solution institutionalized faster than I could by myself, but no one was willing to partner with me on that endeavor. I took the courses alone and published the solutions to the combat-zone logistical issue.

A few months later, I deployed again to Iraq and Afghanistan. One day as I settled down for the day in our compound on a forward operating base in Iraq, the results of the master sergeant promotion board were made public. I had left the idea of promotion with God a long time before, so I had forgotten about the board convening. That day was a real *Oh yeah!* moment for me. I'd been more focused on the task at hand, and it felt good to realize I had my priorities in proper order.[6] Matthew 6:30–33 (AMP) revealed to me the order of importance for things in my life. Even now, I prioritize my efforts according to that scripture.

But if God so clothes the grass of the field, which today is alive and green and tomorrow is tossed into the furnace, will He not much more surely clothe you, O ye of little faith? Therefore, do not worry and be anxious, saying, what are we going to have to eat, or, what are we going to have to drink, or, what are we going to have to wear? For the Gentiles wish for and crave and diligently seek all these things, and your heavenly Father knows well that you need them all. But seek (aim at and strive after) first of all His kingdom and His righteousness (His way of doing and being right) and then all these things taken together will be given you besides.

I knew that my conduct was in line with His expectations for me and that He knew what I needed. If I went about His business, He'd go about providing me my needs and desires.[7] That told me what my disposition should be between the time I asked and the moment God added those things to my life.

In 2010, I was one of 846 sergeants first class eligible for only thirty-three promotions army-wide that year. I became the 29th selected for master sergeant and the only sergeant first class in my organization to be promoted that year, my first year of eligibility. My career was being guided by the Lord in such a way that made me more than eligible for selection to master sergeant long before I was in position for it. I was led by the Lord to do career-enhancing things as a staff sergeant, two ranks earlier, that did not enhance my potential for promotion to sergeant first class but made me a top-tier candidate for master sergeant as soon as I became eligible. It was no wonder that He wouldn't entertain my question about what to do to become a master sergeant. I had already done the things He wanted me to do.

God is an awesome God. His wondrous ways and love for you will leave you praising Him for what He's done that you could not have done alone.

CHAPTER 9

MY LEADERSHIP 101

LEADERSHIP 101—FROM MY FATHER

Without my realizing it, my father had instilled leadership traits in me well before I left home. I knew early on that I preferred to lead. He taught me that leadership was more about the responsibility of it rather than the so-called privileges or prestige that comes with being a leader. My father also made it clear to me that the decisions of leaders make them responsible for the outcome of many things for many people in their spheres of influence. As leaders, we must be willing to stand tall in the moment of unintended outcomes just as well as we do in times of great success. It's a matter of ownership.

My younger brothers and sisters were the training tools my father used to develop the foundation of my leadership skills. I needed to lead them and keep them safe when they were in my care. My father used my playtimes as leadership training opportunities; upon my getting permission to do something, he would tell me, "Take your little brothers and sisters with you!" Being responsible for their welfare as well as mine heightened the need to be aware of my surroundings. I had to know where they were and who they were playing with and make sure that they played safely at all times. At those times my focus would shift from me desiring to play with my friends to my brothers and sisters achieving their goal of having fun. Bringing them home safe and on time became my initial call to leadership. Years later, when I was a noncommissioned officer, a leader of soldiers in wartime, the call was still there.

The army fostered my advanced levels of training in leadership. Some of the army schools I was sent to were the Primary Leadership Development Course (now called Basic Leaders' Course), Basic Non-Commissioned Officer Course, Advanced Leadership Course, Special Operations Forces Senior Enlisted Course, Jumpmaster School, and the Battle Staff Non-Commissioned Officer Course to mention just a few. During my time in uniform, if you wanted my attention and professional opinion, you needed only to bring up the topic of leadership. So I felt at home as a student in these schools.

My father taught me by his example to approach leadership in an unrelenting way, what I call the bulldog approach. If I needed help, he would give me that, but he never accepted excuses for failure. I learned to figure out how to overcome difficult problems that would prevent the completion of my tasks instead of going to him with the issue.

The sports my father allowed me to play enhanced that ethic. I was a collegiate and freestyle wrestler, and I played football, and the no-quit attitude he instilled in me prompted me to stay calm and be decisive and swift with my actions.

In 1981, my father moved us out of the city to a small town a month after I started eighth grade at my middle school, which we called junior high then. That inspired me to be mature like the senior high schoolers my older brother and sisters were. I was arguably the smallest kid in my junior high school, but I wanted to play a sport. I tried out for the basketball team, but because I was just four foot eight, I felt my chances of making the team were slim to none. While I was on the basketball court during tryouts, I watched the wrestlers doing pull-ups and running up and down the bleachers. That interested me more than basketball because I was a playground kid at heart, and they looked like they were having more fun than I was trying to make the basketball team.

I asked a wrestler friend about wrestling, and he said I should talk to the coach after school. I introduced myself to the coach and instantly felt I was supposed to be a part of what they were doing simply by the way the coach spoke to me. Playing football in the streets or in the dirt (we called it grass) as I did while growing up, I had to be tough. Playing basketball did not reflect the toughness that had been cultivated in me, but wrestling did.

The coach was a famed wrestler out of Iowa State, a wrestling powerhouse in the late '70s, when he was on scholarship there. I told him I wanted to learn to wrestle, and he told me he would teach me the sport and I'd be good at it. I was determined to be the best wrestler I could be. I was accustomed to playing football, so I thought I had the stamina for wrestling, but when I started training with the team, I learned that basketball and football stamina was not the same as wrestling stamina. Coach discovered my lack of that stamina and worked my butt off. I learned what was valuable to a wrestler. Conditioning was nearly at the top of the list because wrestlers who become tired in a match seriously considered quitting.

He taught me and a few other new wrestlers some textbook moves, which was enough to make us think we were wrestlers. On the day of my wrestling debut, we learned that there was no one on the other team close to my 98 pounds. My coach asked me if I really wanted to wrestle that day, and I told him yes. He said that their smallest wrestler was 120 pounds. He told me that he was bigger but if I used my speed, I could catch him. I was hyped. I wanted to pin that guy. Instead, I got beat in a record-breaking eight seconds. I didn't realize that my opponent might be just as fast as I was and have more experience wrestling. The next week, I got pinned again as did all the others who were new to wrestling.

While walking home in the snow after the match, I had a meeting with myself. I knew that if I quit, I'd be just that—a quitter. I wasn't a quitter, so I figured I'd better get very aggressive about learning how to wrestle. Every match I watched up to that point confirmed that I had a lot to learn about wrestling. The next day, I told my coach that I wasn't quitting and that I needed him to show me how not to be pinned.

After that, he spent the last half of every team practice training just me (since all of the other new wrestlers quit). I got a crash course in defense. The training was like drinking water through a firehose, but I had the desire and aptitude to learn how to be a wrestler. Because there was no one in my weight class in the entire district, the coach had me sparring with my teammates all the way up the weight table; two of my heaviest teammates weighed 165. My coach wanted me to be able to handle a 20-pound difference in any match.

I lost that next week, but I wasn't pinned. My determination showed up. I lost only because I didn't score enough points. So the next week, I got a crash course on offensive (point-scoring) moves. I discovered I could wrestle. And confidence showed up!

I began winning matches, but it wasn't until about my sixth or seventh win in a row that opposing wrestlers stopped laughing at me when we showed up for matches. The word got around that I was wrestling up to twenty pounds over my weight class and was on a winning streak. I went on a thirteen-match winning streak my first year of wrestling and ended the season with a 13–3 record, the best on my team.

Wrestling taught me that there would always be opposition coupled with every opportunity. I realized that I'd have to put forth more than the minimum effort, that I had to focus on the how- tos and ignore the what-ifs if I wanted to succeed in life. Early on, I saw that just about everything I desired to have or do was just outside my reach, that obtaining anything would require effort. In school, I had always been considered undersized for whatever I wanted to do, which was usually a sport. When I was six, the kids in my neighborhood towered over me and said I couldn't play football with them because I was too small. I disagreed. I began to study how Lynn Swann and John Stallworth, Pittsburg Steelers' Hall of Fame wide receivers, caught the football on Sundays and then would go in my backyard and work on my catching skills and route running in hopes of getting a shot to play with the bigger kids.

I got my shot the next summer. I got a tryout with a team that was a player short. The captain told me to run a fly, which basically meant to run straight. I shook a defender at the line and caught the ball. From then on, I was always picked to play.

When I entered high school, I wanted to be and believed I should be a varsity starter. I was fast, never dropped a pass, and had no problem tackling anyone of any size because as I saw it, a tackler was simply a wrestler covered with protective padding. The coaches on the other hand had a hard time getting over the fact that I was only four foot eleven and weighed only 120 pounds as a tenth grader. Being small never really bothered me; I didn't think being small was a drawback for football players.

The coaches saw my talent but couldn't get over my size, so they put me on the junior varsity team as a starter. Funny, right? I looked the size of a JV football player, and I was smaller than some of my JV teammates. I was dissatisfied with the idea of playing JV football. I was accustomed to being the smallest player, but I was still placed on a level of play that was more my size.

I had another conversation with myself. My physical appearance was not a true depiction of how I saw myself. Even though I was still shopping for shoes and clothes in the children's section, I saw myself easily as six foot two and two hundred pounds. So when the day of our first JV game came, I was upset about everything. JV games were played on Thursdays instead of under the Friday night lights. We on JV had to wear our hand-me-down jerseys to school on game days. I was upset and embarrassed about all that. I was upset about looking the size of a JV player; I couldn't shake my attitude. But it all gave me a greater incentive to get up to the varsity squad.

My football roots went back to the city streets; playing tackle in the streets was common, and we never played a game without shedding some blood. We thought that was normal. I mean, I had to display physical and mental toughness even when a parked car tackled me after I caught a pass. Not displaying toughness would get you kicked off the team. The only option I had was to ball out and get off the JV team because quitting was clearly not an option.

The JV level of play was not challenging enough for the way I played the game. I played both offense and defense with a level of intensity and toughness that was better suited for varsity play. The JV team we played in our third game boasted a player who in my opinion had no business on a JV team anywhere; he was the size of a varsity player, and he intimidated my JV teammates. That made me angry. The opposing team made him their running back of course.

I pulled my teammates together before the game and gave them the solution to handling this running back—gang tackling. No one would tackle him alone. Every time he'd be tackled, it would be because his legs were tied up and at least five defensive players had teamed up to take him down. It was a great showing from my teammates for the first three-quarters of the game. Being in the safety position on defense, I had a lot of tackles that day, but one particular tackle set me free from JV.

By the fourth quarter, the score was 6–26. That running back had scored all their touchdowns. On the game-ending drive, they called another run play. As the safety, I was deep near the end zone keeping up with the deepest wide receiver when I saw my teammates wanting no part of tackling that guy anymore. He was headed toward the end zone when I began my pursuit. He turned his attention and direction toward me instead of trying to beat me to the end zone for another touchdown. My teammates saw no reason to prevent another touchdown; the game was ending, and we were already losing by twenty. But I wanted my teammates to draw courage and strength from my effort for the next game. I had motivated them before the game started like Ray Lewis would have to get their courage up. I had to show them what I had been talking about. I got between the running back and the end zone and flat-footedly waited for him near the three-yard line. When he got to me, I scooped him up and put him on his back at about the five-yard line.

They scored on the next play, but the next day, I got outfitted with a varsity team uniform and played under the Friday night lights for the next three years though I didn't break five feet until the end of that school year.

Throughout my career in the army, I faced many mental, physical, and academic challenges, and I always remembered what my father had taught me about facing them. He'd taught me to give everything my best effort and pursue success at only the highest level.

For instance, the Army Physical Fitness Test has a clearly defined scoring table. You know how well you must perform to pass the test, but I never focused on passing it; I focused on achieving the top score and staying at that level. Other soldiers would ask me what they needed to do to just pass the test, but those were generally the ones who performed poorly on test day and attracted the type of attention from their NCOs that they didn't want to attract. I strove for excellence in everything I put my hands to. Some called me an overachiever, but that was okay. I always did my best if for no other reason than to inspire others, to be a leader who was willing to stand out front as the example.

Had it not been for my father and those who set the bar high for me in my early days of soldiering, I would not have realized my many shortcomings. I would've been as many soldiers are who think their leaders are trying to set the bar too high for them, but I was blessed to have had a few leaders who set the bar high for me based on their assessment of my potential. Through what my generation's old-school army leaders called intrusive leadership, they would candidly explain to me what my shortcomings were, how to fix myself, what would happen if I didn't deal with the issues, and how far my career could go if I overcame them. That was all I needed to know.

As a young, recently promoted sergeant, I thought I was ready for being promoted to staff sergeant simply because I was working in a staff sergeant's duty position. When I spoke to my platoon sergeant about recommending me for promotion, she exercised the brand of leadership I mentioned above by simply telling me that I wasn't ready. Her statement rattled my brain that entire day. I finally caught up with her late that day to ask her where I was coming up short and what to do about it so I would be ready. She told me what my shortcomings were, how to overcome them, and what attributes of leadership I had to develop and why. I was very grateful for her mentorship. I was determined to be the best leader of soldiers I could be; I needed only to be pointed in the right direction.

I made every adjustment she suggested not to get her recommendation for promotion but for the sake of becoming a wiser and stronger leader of soldiers. I knew that promotion was an inevitability for me, so my primary thought was to be as prepared for as much responsibility as possible.

No one else in my chain of command was interested in giving me the unadulterated truth. What was really alarming to me after the fact was that had she not just recently arrived at the unit and taken over as my platoon sergeant, I would have been recommended for promotion without having realized my shortcomings. No doubt I would've come up short while having a greater leadership role over more soldiers than before.

A few months later, when she thought I was equipped enough to handle the responsibilities of the next rank without endangering my career or the development of the soldiers I would be leading, she recommended me for promotion. I had trusted her judgment and followed her lead. She helped strengthen me in my weakest areas and prepared me for the promotion board. I was promoted a few months later.

I'm retired from active service, but my dress blue uniform and all the medals and ribbons still speak to me about my career. They tell others where I've been, some of the things I achieved, and what I'm qualified to do. I look at it and remember being only an inch away from being pinned in my fourth wrestling match in my first season. In a split second, I decided that my opponent would not pin me. I discovered a way of escape, took the opportunity, and defeated my opponent. I am also reminded of my uninvited break in military service. Had that reserve unit commander not helped me get back in the army, my additional twenty-five years of service wouldn't have happened.

Looking at my uniform reminds me of finding myself on the brink of losing my career and family. Pondering that had caused me to set aside my finite wisdom and humble myself enough to allow God to turn everything around.

CHAPTER 10

MILITARY LEADERSHIP 201

LEADERSHIP: GOOD, EXCELLENT, OR POOR?

I learned one key rule of life through all my years of service, and that's to never overestimate myself. With my track record of achieving, I knew I could easily fall into a pit of pride, arrogance, and a few other things that are repulsive to those who should be inspired by me. Leaders don't have to put a spotlight on themselves because people are drawn to leadership. Real leaders don't have to make anyone follow them because even the hardest cases are drawn to displays of true leadership.

As a private in my first unit, I was introduced to the unit's baseline standard of performance as a member of a light infantry unit of the Tenth Mountain Division. The standards for tactical and physical fitness alone were so high that at age twenty, I would lie in my bunk after training in tears due the pain I felt. That went on for the first few months because there were also some unwritten rules for soldiers back then. One was that going to sick call, the doctors, to complain about anything was not forbidden but was frowned upon. I was required to express any and all issues first to my first-line supervisor, who happened to be my platoon sergeant, since I was the First Squad leader then. The idea was for the soldiers to develop trust and confidence in their leadership, and what better way to develop that trust than for your supervisor to be the sole source for fixing your problems.

I told him of the issue I was having and asked why I shouldn't go to the doc for help. He told me I would miss training if I did because the doctor would give me a profile—a doctor's recommendation to your commander for no running or ruck marching—which would slow my development down. I thought, *My development?*

My platoon sergeant told me that pain was a part of the process that would allow me to run long distances, rappel down mountainsides and out of helicopters, march for tens of miles, and so on. We were required to ruck march twelve miles within three hours in full combat gear with a thirty-five-pound rucksack and our weapons. My platoon trained up for the twelve-miler by doing one with a fifty-pound rucksack every Wednesday in addition to the physical fitness regimen we conducted throughout the week. If you missed the scheduled ruck march, you made it up on the upcoming Saturday morning. There was also an annual requirement for your brigade to execute a hundred-mile force march over four days. All the training leading up to accomplishing these requirements were done using fifty- to seventy-five pound rucksacks. I received orders to transfer overseas and missed doing my first hundred-miler, but I didn't miss any of the training that led up to it.

My platoon sergeant said I must become aware of what I could do with my body, what the pain levels felt like, and how much energy I had left in my tank after each phase of training. He also taught us the difference between our bodies being hurt and injured and how to apply first aid. I embraced his training process and became very good at all he taught us. He delivered on everything he said. I arrived at that level of tactical and physical fitness excellence he spoke of and exemplified those standards of performance everywhere I went from then on. That is an example of the foundational breeding I was exposed to.

Two years after I was assigned to a new unit, my first platoon sergeant retired. He was a NCO from the Vietnam era who spent two of his last four years pouring into me. After his retirement, in my mind, he left it up to me to carry the torch of excellence. He didn't ask me to, but I willingly took on the responsibility because I knew he had given me all the tools to do so confidently.

After some years, I became a master fitness trainer, master parachutist, and a member of the Sergeant Audie Murphy Club (a membership reserved for the hand-selected top 2 percent of the noncommissioned officers of the US Army). What he bred in me became the new me. Some have labeled it brain-washing, but I call it developing and becoming. I thank God that someone saw enough potential in me to take me beyond the meager image I had of myself to a higher mental and physical state of being that I hadn't known existed in me.

My first platoon sergeant was an example of excellent leadership at that level for me. He epitomized excellence daily. Our lives under his leadership were simple—Just keep up with him, practice, and become good at what he taught us, and we'd meet the expectations. His performance spoke to me, and his professionalism set the bar for me. The way he did everything influenced me. His investment in us was his influencing. I believe that if you're in a position of authority or influence, you are the principal investor in what you want the outcome to be in your sphere of influence. Meaning: you must walk the walk more than you talk the talk!

I often thought that he was fully aware of our watching his every move as young soldiers do and always displayed his best performance daily. I never witnessed him being unprofessional in any way. Once, he dealt with a soldier of our platoon in a very stern way because the soldier was being extremely insubordinate and physically threatening. He then reported on himself to the first sergeant and commander. I watched him stand outside their offices at parade rest for about twenty minutes before he was brought in. I don't know whether he was reprimanded, but that didn't matter. What stood out for me was that he had actually reported what he deemed unprofessional conduct to the chain of command. No soldier would've reported on him. The incident would not have been known outside the platoon had he not reported on himself. I respected his integrity greatly.

Others in my platoon sided with the insubordinate private, but I saw it from the platoon sergeant's perspective. He was leading, and it was our job to follow him. Up until that point, to include that day, our platoon sergeant had given no one any cause to be insubordinate and reject his leadership despite the grueling training regimen he prescribed for us. As a result of the training, our platoon was leading the pack in so many areas of soldiering in our company that we were well respected and expected to always do well. It was primarily due to his leading and guiding, not anyone's individual effort.

I gave my thoughts to the other privates, and they couldn't understand why I would side with someone who was making us run long distances, climb ropes, and do twelve-mile ruck marches within three hours every week. My statements launched a full-blown pity party.

After my leader reported on himself, the insubordinate soldier was transferred to another brigade. A year or so later, he came back to visit. He had been promoted above his peers twice in his new unit. I believed that my platoon sergeant's foundational training led him to outperforming the others in his new unit. I thought he should've thanked our platoon sergeant for conditioning him to operate at such a level. Instead, he came to gloat. I saw in him my platoon sergeant's investment yielding the high dividends he had hoped for.

Young soldiers instinctively rate their leaders as good, excellent, or poor. When I was a young staff sergeant in a new unit for only a few months, I overheard two soldiers who had determined which category I belonged to. One soldier said to the other, who had just arrived at the unit, "If you want to know about anything, don't go to him. Go to Staff Sergeant Ward." That kind of talk I was used to, but the next two statements blessed me and gave honor to God. The other soldier asked, "Isn't he one of those Christians?" The other said, "No. He's a real Christian!" No other award I've received meant more to me than overhearing that exchange.

I am a Christian. I believe in the Lord Jesus Christ. My brand of leadership is grounded in the Word of God. I unashamedly studied the Word of God and let the NCO creed guide me in methods of professional leadership and conduct so that I could be all I should be to everyone around me. God blesses us and expects us to bless others.[1] Being a blessing for others is not an option. To me, it is spreading the love of God. (Chapter 11 better explains what I mean.) My role in other people's lives ought to be an element of enhancement, a benefit to them if you will. I should be an experience that is of good report when thought of.

With humility for what you should be to others, let the power of influence drive your leadership and authority. Draw others by example, not by demand, threats, or intimidation. You can't put leadership on like a shirt. Everyone around you will see clearly whether it's on you or in you. You must become, not just be appointed, a leader. Without mentorship on how to influence others to accomplish tasks and missions, you could easily develop a team that is equipped to do only what you say while lacking the courage to make any decisions on their own for fear of your disapproval or reprisal.

I believe that the power of influence is the answer to shrinking the population of poor leaders. Influencing others to work better, train harder, lead others better, accomplish tasks, and exceed expectations is more than just these results. New and better results can dismantle the culture previously established in any environment. With everyone seeing these new results consistently, you can effectively reset the organization's performance standards and redefine what is actually excellent, good, and unacceptable in any workplace. It will also reset and redefine what the standards are in the heart and mind of everyone who embraces you as their influencer.

POOR LEADERSHIP

Poor leadership can be found everywhere. Most people who are subjected to it simply react emotionally and complain to others. The real question is what to do about it. I am passionate and compassionate about leadership. My passion is in developing leaders. I am compassionate about the relationship between the leaders and those who are being led, and I never forget that future leaders come from the ranks of those who were led. Every atmosphere people find themselves in is a reflection of those who own or manage it.

As a first sergeant, I focused primarily on the development of my NCOs and how they led the soldiers in their care. My assessment of a leader is summed up in the answer to one question: "If a leader has to step away from his or her duty for a time, could their personnel continue to perform, or would the current mission or task fail because of the leader's absence?" Often, leaders do have to step away for a time. This is the self-assessment tool I used on myself even when I was not in charge of anyone else. All leaders should assess themselves in this way without waiting for their leaders' assessments. It will show them how well they have decentralized their responsibilities and show them how well or how poorly they've trained their subordinates and what areas need additional developing. This moment of truth will also tell whether leaders have effectively developed a sense of responsibility in their subordinates.

In some cases when I dealt with leaders on intimate levels, I learned that they would not step away and take care of personal matters because they knew they had not developed their subordinates well enough to be absent. As a senior NCO I targeted these types of shortcomings and developed my NCOs there. Developing the leaders made for swift improvements in their spheres of influence. Today's leaders reflect on tomorrow's in ways most don't realize. It is imperative that they get it right as quickly as possible. This also translates to parenting, which is in my humble opinion the ultimate leadership role.

The biggest fear of some leaders I've known is believing that empowering their subordinates will cause them to become obsolete, unnecessary, or just simply overpaid in the eyes of their bosses. To the contrary (at least in the military), your best opportunity for promotion is in the hands of those you develop and empower. While you're increasing their value in an organization through training and mentorship, their gratitude alone will cause them to shout from the rooftops that you're the best person to be promoted to greater responsibility. Your boss will hear it louder and clearer coming from them than from you.

HOW I TRANSCENDED

Being exposed to many different brands of leadership helped me become a leader. As is the case with many others, I emerged from the ranks of those who were led and became a leader. Even before the days of being a private, I had a passion for leadership. I experienced many types of leaders with their own or canned (textbook) approaches to mission accomplishment and was exposed to a variety of leadership styles. Despite having to decipher most and wade through the rest of the demonstrations of leadership, I held true to the foundational description of full-spectrum leadership my father had taught me. It helped me keep my roles and responsibilities to my superiors and subordinates at the forefront of my mind. I disregarded the types of leadership that didn't line up with my father's example, the Word of God, or the NCO creed (which basically sums up the other two).

I learned that soldiers want to soldier well. When I observed them long enough, I saw that in them. I decided early in my career that I would take that longer look at all fellow servicemembers to discover their hidden potential. I operated on the principle that there was a treasure, a worth, a value in everyone, but at times, it needed to be brought to the light. That's where leadership comes in.

There are plenty of people in the world whose talents you can see from a mile away, but others' talents aren't always that visible. When I was just a playground kid, I always rooted for the underdog. I would deliberately pick people to play on my team who weren't from popular groups. In a lot of cases, my teammates and I would be laughed at until we started playing against other teams. Then our opponents would see that it wasn't necessarily important to be good individually; it's more important to be good collectively.

Because I understood that, I'd quickly find the talent in each of my teammates and organize them into a team that had a chance of winning. I'd make sure they knew that I believed in each of them, and before we'd play, I'd make sure they knew that I wanted to win and that we could win but only by leaning on each other's abilities. I would ask for their commitment, and they would give it. In most of these cases, our ragtag teams won about half the time, but in all cases, we gave the other teams a serious run for their money. It's always an exhilarating feeling when I can help unleash others' talents and cause them to be recognized and respected. People are never the same after they discover the value within themselves. So many gifts and talents go unrealized. I thank God for the gift and passion to draw out the talents and gifts in others. There are treasures in these earthen vessels we call people, but they have to be discovered. It is this discovery that changes their lives.

I recall a young soldier brought to me by the executive officer of my battalion back in 2005. The soldier was reassigned from a company to my higher-echelon staff. We were about two months away from a deployment to Iraq. The transfer was a confidence-crushing blow to this soldier. My senior leader's demand was that I "fix the soldier's issue" and get him back in his position. I knew that everyone had value and that I simply needed to find out what his was and put him in a place where his value could shine.

I asked him what he wanted to gain from his army experience. He said he had joined to serve his country because of 9/11. He said he met all the physical fitness requirements for his duty assignment, but because of a minor medical issue, which didn't affect his performance, he was taken off the team and sent to my staff. I asked him if he really wanted to get back on his team, and he said no. I told him what I was expected to do. I knew he had something under the hood, some ability, gift, or talent that would benefit the entire organization at the staff-level while we were deployed. I asked him to tell me about himself. By the time he and I finished talking, I was so excited about my new soldier who had been dropped in my lap that I called my wife on my way home and told her to put a pot of coffee on because I had a story to tell.

Back then, the largest issues plaguing deploying units were power generation and the lack of construction materials. We had to know how to get maximum and sustainable power out of our commercial generators and get the construction materials we needed in a timely fashion. I'd been praying about solving these issues as our deployment departure date drew near. The Lord gave me favor with those who controlled the budget for the entire task force and those at the higher echelon who managed the shipping containers. I was given an additional twenty-foot shipping container and stocked it with 40k worth of construction materials that I purchased locally rather than having to go through the burdensome army procurement system in the combat theater.

But we still had a power problem. It can get up to 130 degrees Fahrenheit in the Middle East, and without consistent power generation, there would be no A/C, no computers, no lights, and no swift information sharing. I found out that my new soldier had left his profession as a licensed electrician (making $80k a year no less) to join the army as an infantryman (making $30k). You think God was answering my prayer concerning my task forces' foreseen power problem by putting such a talented person in my hands? This young private showed me how to get maximum output from our commercial generators and how to properly distribute the power. I needed some additional hardware to handle the distribution. I pitched the solution to the foreseen power generation problem and received another blank check to buy whatever I needed.

Once we arrived in theater and established the power generation for the task force's command center and headquarters, I used my soldier's talent to solve six other battalions' power generation issues, and they were very impressed with the output (especially the company he had been reassigned from). He received an impact award for his service outside his duty as an infantryman. Within two months, he became the most sought-after soldier in our task force.

There's treasure in everyone, and leaders should take the time to uncover the gifts and talents. Some might say, "I don't have time for that. I have too much to do!" I get it. But smart distribution and decentralization of duties and responsibilities are necessary for success in any leader's area of responsibility. Those who don't take time to uncover their subordinates' talents could be ignoring the solution to their "not enough time" problem.

It's always in your best interest to get to know (I'm not talking about making friends with) those who work for and with you and most important their hidden capabilities and potential. You'll have to trust that decentralization will work; it takes being bold and trusting, but for the sake of the operation you're responsible for plus everyone else's growth and career progression, decentralizing the workload is essential. Decentralization is nothing more than delegation. I use the word *decentralization* to help me remember that regardless of whom I delegate a task to, I'm still ultimately responsible for its success or failure. In the army, leaders, not their subordinates, are reminded of that mostly in the moments of failure.

During my days of being a military leader, there were eleven principles of leadership I studied and got to know very well. One was to employ your personnel within their capabilities (which implies that you must find out what they're capable of). I took them all to heart, but that one stuck out for me more the first time I cracked open the army leadership manual. As a young soldier, I desired to do and be responsible for more, but my supervisor wouldn't let go of some of his responsibilities for fear that they wouldn't be completed correctly or in a timely manner. I eventually discussed the issue with him, and he loosened his grip. I refused to let him down seeing that he had agreed to trust me. I'm sure your select personnel will feel the same way if you entrust something important to their care.

I learned a long time ago that if you focused on your subordinates' success, your success will follow. Many of the military enlisted leaders I've known or were acquainted with thought that their promotions were due to their personal hard work. That is probably true for junior subordinates or even young leaders, but that belief should not bleed into the senior ranks of management. With promotion comes a greater need to decentralize your duties as a leader.

The army during my early years cross-trained its personnel so they could handle their counterparts' duties and responsibilities, and I believe that should go for senior leaders as well. At every level of leadership, I would find those with the most potential to assume my leadership role and cross-train them to my position. As a first sergeant, my command sergeants majors understood this principle, and I was required to assume some of their duties as well. We knew we might not be able to be everywhere we were expected to be or even present for duty every day. Over my army career, one thing remained true: whatever mission or task that was expected to happen that day was going to happen with or without you. If you were a part of the executing team but unable to do your part, you had better have someone in your place who could. That's where cross-training comes in. That was the army way during my days.

From my days as a private and on, I understood the importance of personnel development. As an NCO, I found it very difficult to fail any mission if I decentralized and cross-trained. In my first two unit assignments, we had to be proficient in two other military occupations—one being of combat arms and the other being a support function. We were tested twice a year on our technical and tactical proficiency in the two cross-trained occupations including our primary military occupational specialty. Being bred in that manner expanded my capacity to learn and do more.

CHAPTER 11

LEARNING TO WALK IN LOVE

While facing the challenges that came up in my marriage, I prayed for God to deliver my family and me from divorce and the despair that surrounded us. In less than a week, He answered my prayer. It was done. I packed my family up a couple of months later, and we moved to our new duty assignment in Chicago. Immediately, the clouds in our lives began to scatter. My new assignment gave me more time to spend with my family and helped strengthen our bonds of love.

I'd been accustomed to arriving at my office at four in the morning and working until eight or nine in the evening. I once tried to leave the office (undetected) at seven, but I was seen, called into the office, and asked a question that took me two hours to answer. My family would always be right where I had left them—in bed. In my new assignment, however, I had to leave the office at four thirty or risk being locked in by security. And weekend work didn't exist. I got to spend much more time with my family, which was wonderful.

There was only one problem with it all: I'd made a vow to God in prayer when everything seemed lost and I had nowhere else to turn, but I hadn't upheld my part of the agreement. He started petitioning my heart to collect.

THE RETURN

A couple of months after we settled into our new life in Chicago, I was in my cubicle and felt the presence of the Lord arrest my heart. He asked me one question: *So are you going to do what you said?* When the Lord speaks to you, you know it. And I knew what He was asking about—my vow to be His forever. On every occasion, He had swiftly done everything I had asked Him and in a better fashion than I had asked for. I saw that His dealings with me were adding up to His expressing a loving interest in me. I had never felt such an overwhelming presence of love as I felt that moment. I felt I was under a cloak of His love, and I wanted more of it! I was convinced that my life would turn out better with His love than without it. So I said yes to Him. I declared that I would lead a life that gave glory and honor to Him. I didn't yet know what that meant, but that's what came up in my heart and out of my mouth. As the years went on, He has led me by His Holy Spirit into becoming and displaying exactly that.

After that moment in my cubicle, I had questions many of which I hadn't gotten answers to before when I walked out on God in my early teens. If I had gotten those questions answered then, there was no telling how many issues I might have avoided. I needed to close the gaps in my understanding. My top question was concerning what Jesus said about this love thing. Today, I know what He means, but back then, I just couldn't grasp it. With all my heart, I wanted to walk in love toward others, but I didn't understand how that was possible. I knew the scriptures that commanded us to do so. Ephesians 5:2 reads, *"And walk in love, as Christ also hath loved us, and hath given himself for us an offering and a sacrifice to God for a sweetsmelling savour."* But I had never heard anyone preach or teach about love. My father had taken us to many churches, but in them all, every sermon seemed to have the same message: if you don't get saved today, you're going to live a life of eternal damnation.

At the beginning of my parents' walk with Christ, we went to church every day, and there was hardly any teaching on what to do or how to navigate this new life in Christ. There were only sermons about the dos and don'ts, and the only thing I heard on the topic of love was to "pray for those who despitefully use you"[1] and "if someone slaps you on one cheek, turn and give them the other one."[1] At least that's the way I understood the sermons. Luke 6:27–31 reads,

But I say unto you which hear, Love your enemies, do good to them which hate you, Bless them that curse you, and pray for them which despitefully use you. And unto him that smiteth thee on the one cheek offer also the other; and him that taketh away thy cloak forbid not to take thy coat also. Give to every man that asketh of thee; and of him that taketh away thy goods ask them not again. And as ye would that men should do to you, do ye also to them likewise.

I tried getting a better and deeper understanding on my own, which was difficult because I was using the King James Version of the Bible as a boy. As I read the Bible,[1] I got some understanding of the passage. The only problem was that it conflicted with what was taught to me by my parents before they were converted and by my older brothers, sisters, and cousins—You do not turn the other cheek. You don't pray for them. You treat them as they just treated you. But as I read it,[1] it kept coming up that I was to love my enemies and turn my cheek. In my heart, I knew I had my instructions, but I also had firsthand experience that no one would ever do the same for me. The younger kids in my neighborhood were frequently unfriendly.

As much as I tried to resist it, I felt pressure to conduct myself in the same ugly ways just to have the opportunity to play with the other kids. If you acted too friendly (soft as we called it), you would be targeted by unfriendly kids. The hardest situation I had to live through as a kid was when I came home without my ball, which other kids had taken, and my parents would make me go and get it from whoever had it. In my heart, I desired to love, but I felt I needed to harden my heart to protect myself and my belongings.

As the years went on, everything got worse. As the kids my age grew up, they went from harsh words to fistfights and then to gunfights. I had no clue how to obey the law of love under these conditions. I knew that the way I understood love would surely expose me to the same treatment those who couldn't defend themselves received. I needed to be tough.

MY FIRST REAL LOVE WALK CHALLENGE

In all my years of wearing the facade of a tough kid, I had the most trouble with how terrible I felt after doing something that hurt or embarrassed someone. These acts greatly opposed what was in my heart. I also didn't want my younger brothers and sisters to ever feel unsafe while they played, so I watched over them like a lion watches over his pride. They needed to be able to protect themselves after I left home.

In eleventh grade, I revisited the law of love. I asked the Lord to forgive me for my most recent acts (fights at the park and maliciously defending my siblings), and I committed to living according to this command. A few days later, I experienced the fallout of one of my recent altercations. I had an unctioning in my heart to avoid walking down a certain street that would reignite the altercation, but I didn't listen. My decision to continue to walk in love was greatly challenged when I was face to face with someone I had disrespected days before. It was a pivotal moment. I knew that if I didn't honor my commitment to walk in love, my actions outside of love could've very well changed the trajectory of my life.

Looking into his eyes as he faced off with me, I knew that one if not both of us would end up hospitalized if not dead. I quickly made a decision in my heart, and an overwhelming level of compassion came over me. I could have hugged him. I told him I respected him and was truly sorry for what I had done to him. Everyone else there criticized me for my supposedly cowardly words. We walked away from each other and allowed love to prevail as it always does. I sensed that he believed my words because he could tangibly detect the love of God that was engulfing us in that moment. Our friendship was restored and strengthened instantly. The trajectory of our lives could've been altered that day, but the conquering presence of love destroyed any possibility of that. And because God is love, He gets all the glory for it.

I asked God to explain what had happened to me, and He referred me to the law of love. I had an example of what it meant to turn the other cheek. But I didn't understand why I had to experience being humiliated by the onlookers. That neighborhood was like a shark tank. If they smelled fear, you'd have to run to safety the rest of your days. I felt that would be my fate once the word got around.

I didn't get an answer to my pitiful question, but what came up in me was an image of Jesus carrying His cross. I asked Him to forgive me for grieving over feeling humiliated. I was concerning myself with the opinions of others, which truly don't matter when you're doing what's right before God. Sometimes, it's not easy to do the right thing when you consider the pressure of popular opinion. I knew that it was God's will in this instance for me not to defend myself but to forgive him and ask him for forgiveness. For the first time, I had walked in love toward someone who became my enemy. I didn't know what to think about it, but I was glad that I then knew what to do in situations like that. I had exercised wisdom and maturity. Does obeying the law of love mean you will never face opposition? No. Does obeying it mean you're soft? No. I learned that allowing love to prevail in situations like that will bring about the best outcomes for everyone involved.

THE TRANSGRESSION

Back to my miracle assignment in Chicago. All was going well, and many opportunities were coming my way. Greater responsibilities were being given to me. My name was becoming well known as the command was responsible for missions from coast to coast. There seemed to be no one who disliked me.

Then it happened. I began to experience some persecution[2] that seemed to come out of thin air and from multiple directions. I was determined to maintain an honorable, professional approach to everything, but as the days and weeks went on, the challenge to that increased.

My wife and I had recently become members of our church where the pastor was preaching a series on righteousness. I began to understand that I was in right standing with God and began to acknowledge my covenant rights as a Christian. I began to understand that I had authority over the plots and schemes of the enemy[2] as it says in Luke 10:19: "*Behold, I give unto you power to tread on serpents and scorpions, and over all the power of the enemy: and nothing shall by any means hurt you.*" And I was gaining an even deeper understanding of the truth that no one conspiring against me would succeed[3] as is stated in Isaiah 54:17: "*No weapon that is formed against thee shall prosper; and every tongue that shall rise against thee in judgment thou shalt condemn. This is the heritage of the servants of the Lord, and their righteousness is of me, saith the Lord.*"

As I meditated on these things, I realized I had kingdom authority in the place where God had strategically placed me. My eyes of spiritual understanding were being enlightened to what was going on all around me. I began to pray about things that the Holy Spirit would point out to me. He would especially have me pray for those whom I worked for and with.

Later, I received an opportunity to apply for another special assignment. Some of my peers and superiors encouraged me while others sought to discourage. I was accustomed to discouraging words meant to cause me to abandon my dreams. I was saying I will while some were saying I won't, but they didn't know all that I had overcome. I was not one to walk away from an opportunity I desired, and I certainly wasn't going to allow anyone to tell me what I could and couldn't do.

I had to turn my back on those who opposed me and focus on obtaining the special assignment. I spoke with my immediate supervisor, a marine master gunnery sergeant, who said that he would line up interviews with the senior leaders so I could obtain letters of recommendation from them for my application packet. I interviewed with them all and received nine letters of recommendation from the top officials of the command from the East to the West Coast.

By the regulations, I met all the criteria for the special assignment. I sent a copy of my application to my contact at the approving office, who looked it over for any problems with it before I sent in my official application. He gave me the go-ahead, and I submitted the application, and was accepted.

I was more than excited about my orders to begin transitioning to my new special assignment. But the next day was September 11, 2001. We watched on television as the twin towers came crashing down killing all those people. On September 12, I received notification that the acceptance to my special assignment had been revoked. That was a crushing blow. I was enraged at the attack on my nation and the deaths of so many fellow citizens, but the revocation of my orders was a denial of my personal desire. I wanted that assignment because I desired to be at what I thought was the tip of the spear as a soldier. I also pridefully wanted it because some others had thought I couldn't achieve it. The revoking of my orders meant something, but I was missing what that something was. The action was sharp and swift. I then realized God had a different purpose for me.

In the days and weeks that followed, the military prepared for expected orders to mobilize and deploy. I learned that that was the reason for my revocation order. The Department of Defense policy required that all personnel cease their travels and cancel all permanent changes of station and school attendance that hadn't started. That helped me understand my situation better. It was clear to me that God wanted me in a combat zone, not at another nondeployable special assignment.

Within three months, I received orders to report to a unit due to deploy to Iraq.

CHAPTER 12

WEAPONIZING MY LOVE WALK

I thought I had the love lesson down pat. I couldn't have been more wrong as I transferred to my new unit overseas that was to deploy in six months. Instead of bringing my wife and sons to a foreign country without support for longer than a year, we decided that I'd have another unaccompanied tour.

I stayed in barracks because we were to depart in six months. I did not discern the enemy's attack on me during my first days of in-processing the unit. I would like to say that my responses to the criticisms and sly, public remarks were good or at least professional, but they were not. Day after day, things were said that I thought were meant to antagonize me. By the end of the first week on station, I let go of my peaceful demeanor and professionalism. Those who didn't know I was a Christian, by my conduct wouldn't have believed it if I told them I was. My buttons were pushed, and I responded with, well let's just call them unprofessional statements.

The traditional way soldiers fixed issues between one another back then was to go around the back of the building and fight it out. The only issue with that was that we weren't soldiers. We were leaders of soldiers whose conduct was expected to set an example for others. Before the watchful eyes of other young soldiers, I offered that opportunity to someone who outranked me, which was totally unprofessional. It was a terrible showing by two NCOs who knew better. As soon as I finished delivering the message, my new first sergeant came in the office. I thought I would be chewed out and officially reprimanded being that I, a staff sergeant, had publicly threatened a sergeant first class, but that didn't happen though it would have been just. The first sergeant didn't even look at me.

As the day went on, I became more irritated at the thought of having to do this assignment for the next two years alone. My newborn son was only two weeks old when I had left. I was completely out of control in my thoughts when my wife called that same evening. I didn't want to answer the phone because I knew I wouldn't be able to hide from her what was going on in my mind. I hadn't spoken to her that day, but she didn't greet me the normal way she always did. With a stern voice, she asked, "What are you doing?" I knew the Lord had had her call me knowing that I had basically shut Him out and was set in my mind to do the wrong thing in retaliation for the humiliation I had received from that NCO.

I told her what had happened and how I had decided to fix it. In her patented way of softening my heart, she said, "Baby, you're a man of God. You walk in love toward everyone. Whatever someone said or did to you is not worth what you're intent on doing to him. You know that whatever you're thinking about doing is not the right thing to do."

I told her I needed to get off the phone, and she said to call her the next day. I considered the rightness of her words, and I asked the Father to forgive me and tell me the right thing to do. The Lord said, *Ask that person to forgive you.* I couldn't believe it. I asked, "Why should I ask him for forgiveness? He started it. He should be asking *me* for forgiveness". At that moment I acknowledged my lack of maturity in the whole situation.

But I knew He had said all that He was going to say about the matter. I asked Him, He answered me, and then He dropped the mic.

I had a decision to make; would I be obedient or not? It was as simple as that. I was so drained from the whole ordeal that I fell asleep in my uniform. When I woke up the next morning, the dilemma was right where I had left it, right in front of my face, because I hadn't made a decision.

I put my physical fitness uniform on to go to first formation. There was no way around or out of this issue. The situation was coming to a climax in my heart; I had not decided to obey or disobey God. Then I said, "Father, nothing is worth hindering my relationship with you, so I forgive him, but I need your help to do what you've told me to do."

I walked the two blocks to the formation and saw him standing in front of the platoons, over sixty people present there. I was determined to do what the Father had instructed me to do. As I came near to the NCO to willingly do what the Father directed me to do His presence came over me. I saw the NCO not as an enemy but as the Father saw him. I felt the love God had for him. I knew that if my Father loved him, I should as well.

With everyone looking and listening, I told him, "Sergeant, I don't know what I've done to offend you, but I apologize for it and won't conduct myself in that manner again. Will you forgive me?" All the soldiers heard me and looked at us in disbelief.

Then the unthinkable happened. The sergeant first class started dropping some tears and apologized profusely for how he had spoken to me all week, and he asked for my forgiveness. He told me he hated the way he treated other people; he said he'd be a better leader than he'd been from that point on.

Praise God! I could not have witnessed a bigger victory than that. He stopped treating me and others the way that caused many to loathe him. During my time in that unit, no one ever experienced problems with him like that again. The true love of God conquered that day.

THE DAWN OF WEAPONIZED LOVE

It dawned on me that God's love had destroyed the plots and schemes of the enemy by exercising His love in a hate-charged atmosphere. I began to see love as a weapon that annihilated anything that did not originate from heaven. Ever since I could remember, I questioned why it seemed Christians had to embrace martyrdom to walk in love. In my heart, I strongly disagreed with martyrdom, but at the same time, it seemed as though we simply misunderstood the command to love our enemies[1] as said in Matthew 5:43–44.

Ye have heard that it hath been said, thou shalt love thy neighbor, and hate thine enemy. But I say unto you, love your enemies, bless them that curse you, do good to them that hate you, and pray for them which despitefully use you, and persecute you.

I realized that God's love conquered fear and hate just as light conquers darkness.

WHAT IS LOVE?

The Bible says that God is love.[2] In 1 John 4:16, we read, *"And we have known and believed the love that God hath to us. God is love; and he that dwelleth in love dwelleth in God, and God in him."*

Knowing that God is love explained so many of my experiences that had been mysteries to me. When God's love fills your heart and you allow Him to dictate your actions and attitudes, it's very difficult to operate in the world's hateful ways. I had to leave God in order to match hate with hate. God is love! He is the supreme force that dwells in me. He is with me and will never fail me or forsake me[3] as Joshua 1:5 says: *"There shall not any man be able to stand before thee all the days of thy life: as I was with Moses, so I will be with thee: I will not fail thee, nor forsake thee."* It says that there shall not be any man able to stand before you all the days of your life.[3] As God's love was with Moses, so would it be with me. The issues that come up against you really aren't a match for you if you're walking a true love walk with God.

On the battlefields of problems, issues, and altercations, by walking in love you bring to bear the full magnitude of the Father Himself. Deuteronomy 20:4 (AMP) tells us, *"For the Lord your God is He Who goes with you to fight for you against your enemies to save you."*

In medieval times, I believe the rules of engagement stated basically that whoever took the battlefield won. Most of us have heard the phrase, "Go with God," right? Consider that God is love, and that He understands His covenant promise to you of never failing you or forsaking you, and also how the apostle Paul (in 2 Corinthians 2:14) thanked the Father, who "always causes us to triumph":[3, 5] *"Now thanks be unto God, which always causeth us to triumph in Christ, and maketh manifest the savour of His knowledge by us in every place."*

If you are a believer, it behooves you to never do battle or business outside of love, without God. According to His Word, He will make you the victor on every field of battle. The moment you engage in conflict without Him, you might forfeit the victory He promises you to the opposing force. Applying the revealed knowledge found in these four scriptures early in my return caused an instant reversal to the patented losses I had been experiencing in my life regularly.

Walk into every engagement in love. That's how you cooperate with God. That's the revelation I found in those scriptures. He revealed Himself in a very different way to my wife than He did to me although He's the same God. I believe His chosen ways are based on our individual designs and purposes. No one knows the fullness of God, but however we come to know Him in the light of the truth, the one common denominator we are all founded upon is that God is love.

The first two months on ground in Iraq (2004) were spent building our infrastructure and surveying our task force's area of responsibility. But with only three months left in the tour, I was told by my commander that I would be awarded a certificate of appreciation for deploying with my unit on a fourteen-month combat tour and for my contributions to the task force's success. I said, "Yes sir," but a certificate of appreciation for an NCO was an improper, disingenuous act of recognition. Most chains of command do not recognize leaders using unit certificates and especially not publicly. Certificates of appreciation in the army are traditionally awarded to privates and specialists, not noncommissioned officers. I could have felt offended, but I knew that was what the enemy wanted, and I refused to walk out of love with anyone. I wanted to stay partners with God. I continued to hold my chain of command and fellow soldiers up in prayer without ceasing.

With one month of my tour remaining, our three-star general came to our compound for a high-level briefing but wanted a tour of the compound first. By the time my battalion and company commanders brought him around to my area, my name had been mentioned to him so many times that he was shockingly excited to meet me. I had not been expecting any generals to visit that day or any other day for that matter. I gave him a tour of my area of responsibility and explained to him why I had set the operation up that way. I told him that I had the new task force that would replace us in mind. I wanted a seamless handover of all the buildings, combat equipment, munitions, and supplies so they could take over the mission immediately.

He was so impressed with what he heard that he told my company and battalion commanders, "Give this NCO a Bronze Star. Have the paperwork on my desk to sign by the end of the week." The general elaborated a bit more about my contributions to the task force and how my efforts tied into the overall success of the entire organization as they departed my office. I was not really aware of how the Lord had guided my efforts until that moment, but all the glory belongs to Him.

Multiple times during that deployment, the Holy Spirit would show me certain issues and explain or have someone else explain to me how the issues frustrated the task force's missions and how to fix them. For example, the Lord led me to two abandoned 500 kW Cummins generators, which I had two five-ton trucks bring to our compound. I had them set them up so they would run six hours each and be off for six hours so they wouldn't overheat. That gave us power twenty-four hours a day whereas before, we'd have to shut down our generators and thus cut all electricity for six hours at a time to allow them to cool down. The Lord blessed me so that I could be a blessing like that throughout the deployment. I was grateful to have received that Bronze Star, but I knew that walking in God's love was responsible for that. It will turn every situation around and cause even your enemies to be at peace with you.[9] Proverbs 16:7 says, "*When a man's ways please the Lord, he maketh even his enemies to be at peace with him.*"

Love positions you for the goodness of God to operate in, through, and for you unrestrictedly. His will is done through you and to you if you are walking in love. His will is always from a heart full of love because He is love. I was obedient in love to stand in the gap for my fellow soldiers. God had positioned me there knowing I would obey His Word, which enabled us to finish the combat tour without losing a single soldier. I still feel honored to have been His instrument to do His will in the lives of others.

God is love, and the accounts of my life (people call them miracles) are His true acts in love. Tornados, earthquakes, and hurricanes are not acts of God. Those are acts that derive from hate, which is counter to the character of God, which is love. If you're experiencing something that is outside of the realm of love no matter how miniscule it is, be aware that satan is the originator of it, not God. I equate love to a weapon, and I operate in my life (in this hate-charged world) by using it to destroy the work of the devil.

God's love has always made me triumphant in every situation. My love walk has been weaponized, and I am free to express the love of God in every situation as the Lord directs me. That became evident to me the many times He sent me to different places for love's sake. Because I committed myself to obeying His law of love, He was having me do great exploits for Him. I have been placed in so many critical positions throughout my life, and whenever I look back, I see God's signature in all of those moments. I know that this love thing ignites so many opinions about God and emotions from one end of the spectrum to the other, but God loves us and wants us reconciled to Him. That's why He sent Jesus. John 3:16 says, *"For God so loved the world, that He gave His only begotten Son, that whosoever believeth in him should not perish, but have everlasting life."*

I begin every endeavor anticipating His intent in it as He is my only employer. In my house, we confess that we are blessed and will be a blessing everywhere we go and in everything we do. That's why we are always in the right place at the right time. Even the youngest of my sons understands that a simple trip to the store is not always just for purchasing something, that he represents his family as an ambassador of Christ. When any of us go out among those in the world, we know that it's always an event not to be taken lightly. We must avail ourselves of the loving work of God. I did not say to go out and create opportunities. That's what God does. While you cooperate with God, experiencing you might be the catalyst others need to turn their hearts to the Lord.

RIGHTLY DEFINING LOVE IN YOUR LIFE

In recent times, because I was prayed up and my faith was built up in the Word, I was able to assume the believer's proper position of dominion over whatever confronted me. Praise God for loving us enough to give us dominion over situations and circumstances. You might say, "God doesn't treat me like that" or "He hasn't done that for me." It's not my place to judge anyone's walk of faith, but God is not a respecter of persons. As Peter said in Acts 10:34 (AMP), *"And Peter opened his mouth and said: Most certainly and thoroughly I now perceive and understand that God shows no partiality and is no respecter of persons."*

If you are a born-again believer, He's positioned you the same way regardless of what your experiences have led you to believe.[13] That was done by His love for us all, and there's no variance or levels of

His love. God is one thing: love.[14] His love isn't conditional as some people's love is. Misunderstanding this or believing God is like people might be the issue many of my brothers and sisters in Christ have. They may be defining love wrong. No dictionary truly or completely defines love.

The Word of God speaks for itself. God is love! Some people may know only certain byproducts of love and believe that is the entirety of its definition. Defining love through the conduct of others is a big mistake. So many hearts have been broken based on falsely defining the actions of those some believed met the letter of the definition but were found to be untrue and maybe even untrustworthy. This is possible because every defining statement about love in the dictionary is centered around emotions and physical acts. Love is not physical acts or emotions. Love is spiritual. Love is God. Love is a person, not a feeling.

Over the years, many fellow soldiers and some officers asked my advice on their marital or other relationship problems. They would see me and my family and assume we had a great family life and marriage. The most common issue was love lost, unfortunately common in so many marriages especially in the military community. Whenever I sat down with couples or individuals, I first told them that they would receive from me some very unconventional answers. Then I would ask them to commit to settling in their hearts that it was possible to restore their relationship and even make it better despite the way they felt about each other at that time. I know from personal experience that true solutions to marital issues will challenge you in ways you can't imagine.

I often chuckle at how many issues my wife and I have overcome in our twenty-five-plus years of marriage. But God, Love, showed us the way every time. His Word also shows us as husband and wife, as parents, and as individuals how to become stronger than ever. So I would give those whom I counseled testimonials from my life as they pertained to their issues, highlight the wisdom I had gained, and tailor it to their situations.

When it came to falling out of love, I told them that love should not depend on someone's independent definition of it. It was always an epiphany experience when I would explain that God was the love that they should love each other with. I told them to love each other with God's love or better yet love each other with God instead of by themselves alone. I believe that you need God's love to love anyone properly. It has always been God's plan for us to cooperate with Him in every aspect of life.

I would remind those who sought my advice that at one point in the past, they were intrigued by the other and wanted to know more about him or her and the attraction felt. But after they married or had children, the pressures of life would come upon them and cause them to forget what they had learned about each other, why they wanted to be in each other's lives. The tendency is to focus more on those life issues instead of coming into the knowledge of the force of unity they could have together that no circumstance could overpower.

Genesis 1:27 tells us, "*God created man in His own image, in the image of God created He him; male and female created He them.*" As our Creator, He knows us better than our parents do. He knows things about us that are yet to be unveiled. I tell married couples that they received backstage passes to each other's lives. I believe most people simply aren't prepared for what goes on backstage in marriage.

I tell married men that their wives were the best thing that they ever added to their lives; all they had to do was ask the Creator, not their parents or friends. Only their Creator knows what He designed their wives to do and be and how they function. It's a lack of understanding that causes couples to exhaust their love for each other.

The Father's love is inexhaustible! So if you ran out of love (or fell out of love), it is obvious that you were using the wrong love. God is love, so the only way for love to be restored to your heart is to get Him in your heart. The Father will show you what to love about your spouse and how to love them. He did that for me.

The enemy has been diligent in showing you what not to like, but what does that have to do with real love? The Father will show you how to see your spouse. Proverbs 31:10–31 (AMP) tells husbands what they will see in their wives beyond what they thought they knew about them.[15]

A capable, intelligent, and virtuous woman—who is he who can find her? She is far more precious than jewels and her value is far above rubies or pearls. The heart of her husband trusts in her confidently and relies on and believes in her securely, so that he has no lack of [honest] gain or need of [dishonest] spoil.

She comforts, encourages, and does him only good as long as there is life within her. She seeks out wool and flax and works with willing hands [to develop it]. She is like the merchant ships loaded with foodstuffs; she brings her household's food from a far [country].

She rises while it is yet night and gets [spiritual] food for her household and assigns her maids their tasks. [see Job 23:12.] She considers a [new] field before she buys or accepts it [expanding prudently and not courting neglect of her present duties by assuming other duties]; with her savings [of time and strength] she plants fruitful vines in her vineyard. [see Song of Solomon 8:12.]

She girds herself with strength [spiritual, mental, and physical fitness for her God-given task] and makes her arms strong and firm. She tastes and sees that her gain from work [with and for God] is good; her lamp goes not out, but it burns on continually through the night [of trouble, privation, or sorrow, warning away fear, doubt, and distrust].

She lays her hands to the spindle, and her hands hold the distaff. She opens her hand to the poor, yes, she reaches out her filled hands to the needy [whether in body, mind, or spirit]. She fears not the snow for her family, for all her household are doubly clothed in scarlet.

She makes for herself coverlets, cushions, and rugs of tapestry. Her clothing is of linen, pure and fine, and of purple [such as that of which the clothing of the priests and the hallowed cloths of the temple were made].

Her husband is known in the [city's] gates, when he sits among the elders of the land. She makes fine linen garments and leads others to buy them; she delivers to the merchants girdles [or sashes that free one up for service].

Strength and dignity are her clothing and her position is strong and secure; she rejoices over the future [the latter day or time to come, knowing that she and her family are in readiness for it]!

She opens her mouth in skillful and godly Wisdom, and on her tongue is the law of kindness [giving counsel and instruction]. She looks well to how things go in her household, and the bread of idleness (gossip, discontent, and self-pity) she will not eat.

Her children rise up and call her blessed (happy, fortunate, and to be envied); and her husband boasts of and praises her, [saying], Many daughters have done virtuously, nobly, and well [with the strength of character that is steadfast in goodness], but you excel them all. Charm and grace are deceptive, and beauty is vain [because it is not lasting], but a woman who reverently and worshipfully fears the Lord, she shall be praised! Give her of the fruit of her hands, and let her own works praise her in the gates [of the city]!

As I read these passages, I saw the mystery of my wife unfold before my eyes. It was internally embarrassing to discover how many things about her I didn't understand and thought were hinderances to our marriage. Even my career in the military thrived largely because of these attributes, which she was operating in. Once my eyes were opened, I became quite appreciative of my exclusive backstage pass to her life. Don't love your woman the way the world does; love her the way God, her Creator, does. You'll see her in ways you've never seen any woman.

Some I spoke with initially did not believe they were capable of meditating on those scriptures as I did, but they vowed to try. Most of them witnessed transformations in their hearts that caused them to correlate what the scriptures said and what they saw in their wives. They came to realize that the issue was with themselves primarily, which put them in a dominant position to overcome their marital and relational issues because they were internal rather than external.

Operating in love in any situation is to apply God to it. It may seem like a weak posture in hostile moments, but that's only because God would have you apply what the world would call a foolish approach to establish your victories in life.[16] In 1 Corinthians 1:27, we read, *"But God hath chosen the foolish things of the world to confound the wise; and God hath chosen the weak things of the world to confound the things which are mighty."*

God rules over all. He is the judge,[17] and He was spoken of in Psalm 75:7 and Psalm 103:19.

But God is the judge: he putteth down one and setteth up another.

The Lord hath prepared his throne in the heavens; and his kingdom ruleth over all.

We can bring the judge to the battlefield of every skirmish. Whose side will He judge in favor of if you brought Him to the battle? Plenty of people would love to have judges in their pockets, but believers have *the* judge as their abiding friend who wants to be closer to them than anyone else does.

Weaponizing your love walk is necessary especially in these latter days when conditions on earth are getting worse.[18] Love is not a weapon of the flesh but of the spirit that destroys everything contrary to it.[19] It goes over the high walls people have built up to safeguard themselves, and it wages war at the root of every issue.

CHAPTER 13

THE DEPLOYMENTS WERE GOD'S WILL

My deployments to various theaters of operation (Kuwait, Iraq, Afghanistan, Philippines) were of the upmost importance to God. His purpose was in the work He had for me to do there. I did not understand that until after the first couple of months of my first deployment to Iraq in 2004.

Nothing was really established over there at least as far as most of us had expected. The mission of my unit was to patrol and safeguard the main supply routes (MSRs) meant to secure logistical support for all the units in the combat theater. The mission was an honorable one, but there was a glaring issue with it; we didn't have adequate equipment to fulfill it. That was where my mission within the unit's mission began. We arrived twelve months after the military campaign in Iraq began, but we were told to expect to be in-country for the better part of eighteen months before we would be relieved.

We had relieved a reserve unit that had been there for twelve months without a single soldier lost. A couple of months after our arrival, they were ordered to resume their mission for an additional six months. It was only after their twelfth month in-country that they began to suffer fatalities. I watched as the morale of that unit fell dramatically. They had been due to get home and resume their civilian lives. A ceremony for their return had already been prepared, and the local news media was going to be there as they came off the plane. Imagine how many hearts were broken and how many children were disappointed. There's no way I could describe what might have gone through the minds of families whose warriors were killed after they had resumed their duties for the additional six months.

Their primary issue wasn't morale or even the extra six months in-country. It was that the insurgents had started using improvised explosive devices (IEDs). These devices seemed to be everywhere. At that time, there were no tactics, techniques, or procedures (TTPs) to address how to defend against IEDs. What was even more alarming to me as we began to be outfitted for our mission were some of the vehicles we inherited from them. We inherited what were called training-shell Humvees framed in fiberglass with sandbags in the floorboards and flak jackets draped over the doors. They were aptly named up-armored Humvees. I couldn't believe we were expected to patrol and transport personnel in vehicles not equipped to bring us back alive. Some of the Humvees had steel plating over the driver and passenger fiberglass doors, which made us feel almost invincible, but they still had gun mounts on the roofs with no protection for the gunners. Such combat platforms as they were called were no match for this new threat.

At the counterinsurgency briefing and training, we received word that in a few months we would be getting the new, true, up-armored combat platforms, but we would assume our mission immediately. We looked like an old-school Western movie with our rifles hanging out of covered wagons.

By the grace of God, I came across a master sergeant I knew from a few years back who had retired from the army and landed the position of director for theater logistics in Iraq; he was accountable for all government property in the country. He knew which units were due to rotate in and out of Iraq and when. I told him of my unit's problem with what I called unsafe combat platforms and that we needed better vehicles faster than a few months from then. He told me I could get whatever I needed to better outfit my units until our new trucks arrived. He told a property specialist to work with me to better equip my unit. I received another blank check.

I returned to our forward operating base (FOB) and informed the battalion executive officer and senior logistics NCO of the opportunity and created a plan to methodically retool the entire battalion. At that point, the only equipment we could count on was the weapons we brought from home station. The first things to replace were the Humvees. My buddy's specialist put me in contact with units that were transferring out and needed to offload their equipment. These units had vehicles that would protect my comrades better than those training Humvees we were driving could. The up-armored version then cannot be compared to the up-armored Humvees the armed forces have today, but the vehicles I got were more suitable for combat than what we were currently in. Oh, how untouchable we felt when we got them.

The only problem we had with those trucks was the lack of freon for the A/C systems. Our TTPs at the time stated that we would have all the windows closed after leaving the base—no problem if you have air conditioning to battle the 130 degrees inside the vehicle. The majority of our Humvees lacked one thing or the other, and they were considered some of the best vehicles in theater. I lost seventeen pounds in the first three weeks there because we lacked A/C in our vehicles. We would freeze bottles of water the night before so they would be drinkable while on mission the next day, but that didn't matter much as the water would be too hot to drink by the time we arrived at our destinations. I began to doubt whether the trucks were a blessing due to the many complaints I heard from those who didn't know I had brokered the upgrade.

During that deployment, I set my alarm for 4:00 a.m. so I could pray. I had an unction in my spirit to do that but didn't realize why until a few years later. Job 38:12 (AMP) speaks about praying about your day to prevent the evil the enemy has laid up for you from happening.[1] The wisdom of the Word of God does not always stare you in the face as you read, but when you study it diligently (Joshua 1:8 talks about meditating on the word of God), the kingdom principles are revealed.

Have you commanded your morning since your days began and caused the dawn to know its place, So that light may get hold of the corners of the earth and shake the wickedness [of night] out of it?

I prayed for my leaders and fellow soldiers, their families, and the mission.[3] If I had the opportunity, I'd see some teams off and tell them whatever was put on my heart not as a chaplain but as a fellow fighting soldier.

THE ATTACKS ON THE MSR

One of my tasks was to coordinate the reception of the battalion's munitions including bullets for our rifles and 9 mm pistols, .50-caliber rounds, grenades, and AT4s. The date was set for our mission. We planned the route to the ammo supply depot, the timing of getting there and leaving, and contingency plans in case we had contact with the enemy. We coordinated close air support, devised a medical evacuation (MEDEVAC) plan, and briefed our commander.

The day came to execute the plan. I awoke and gave honor to God as I usually did, but that day was different. He reminded me of His promise in Isaiah 54:17.

No weapon that is formed against thee shall prosper, and every tongue that shall rise against thee in judgement thou shalt condemn. This is the heritage of the servants of the Lord, and their righteousness is of me, saith the Lord.

I didn't understand why He was reminding me of that. I was not concerned for my life or the lives of those with me. I had put my hope and trust in God for that. Then He took me to a scripture I hadn't seen before, in which Jesus spoke of believers in Him having eternal life and never perishing and no man being able to pluck us out of His hands.[5] It's in John 10:27–30.

My sheep hear my voice, and I know them, and they follow me: And I give unto them eternal life; and they shall never perish, neither shall any man pluck them out of my hand. My father, which gave them me, is greater than all; and no man is able to pluck them out of my father's hand. I and my father are one.

These verses painted an even clearer understanding for me as to why I should not fear. No weapon would be successful against me, and I was the possession of Jesus Christ, which was given to Him by God. My accepting Jesus as my Lord and Savior at age seven ensured that relationship. I believed that; I was fully persuaded that I could go back and forth through danger with an uncompromising faith in God and that what He promised would be the reality in my life. Jesus also said in Mark 11:22, "*And Jesus answering saith unto them, Have faith in God.*"

I brought my team together to review the plan and said that in prayer that morning, I had read scripture that told me that Jesus was in God's hands, I was in Jesus's hands, and they were in my hands. I told them that no one could pluck us out of His hand because He was in God and God was greater than all. Everyone received it; that lifted their hearts. Every truck commander (TC) gave a thumbs-up for their team. We loaded our weapons and departed the base.

On the way, we received a directive over the radio to divert to another forward operating base to meet with a sister unit that was heading to the airbase to be issued munitions. We were to add their three Humvees and a five-ton cargo truck to my convoy. We had to give that unit our radio frequencies and do radio checks, brief its members on all our plans, and assign them positions in our convoy. Since they had never worked with me and my team, they were made to understand the techniques we used to safely and quickly get from one place to another.

The only thing they got right from us was the radio frequencies. We added their trucks to the convoy and departed. We were already running over an hour later than planned. It was a good thing that I had planned to arrive at my destination one to two hours earlier than we were expected. We arrived at the airbase without any issues, but we missed our first appointment time. I spoke to the officer in charge at the ammunition supply depot, who squeezed us in right after lunch. I was grateful but calculated that darkness would fall during our return home, which was a dangerous scenario during that time. I made sure the other team got their issue first so we wouldn't have to wait on them.

About thirty to forty minutes into our return travel down the MSR, the lead vehicle, which was from the unit added to my mission, came upon a civilian dump truck carrying a load of gravel in our line of travel. One of my truck commanders radioed the lead truck commander to get the dump truck out of our path. The gunner got the dump truck driver's attention, and he began to switch lanes, but as the lead vehicle began to pick up speed, the dump truck driver pulled back in front of it and hit his brakes. The dump truck with its heavy load of gravel rolled up over the passenger side of the Humvee collapsing the roof on top of the truck commander and the gunner, who was in the gunner's turret.

We immediately maneuvered our trucks into a defensive posture around the Humvee and extracted the three soldiers from the truck. While a few of my guys dealt with the wounded, two others and I moved on the dump truck. The driver had fled. Seeing that a crowd had begun to form, we cordoned off the whole site and stopped traffic. The TC, gunner, and driver were badly injured. The gunner's forelegs were bent at a 90-degree angle in the unnatural direction, the truck commander's skull was badly fractured, which deformed his face, and the driver was in severe shock having witnessed it all. I had one of my NCOs execute the MEDEVAC plan. We cleared an area for the helicopter to land, popped a smoke grenade, and got those guys out of there.

Once the injured were taken care of, we stripped their vehicle of all sensitive items (radios, weapons, ammunition, etc.) and incinerated the vehicle. It was then dusk. Once we ensured that it was properly destroyed, we reassembled the convoy and continued on.

Less than thirty minutes later, my Humvee, the lead vehicle, hit a buried bomb. We saw a young man with a detonating device a short distance from the road. All glory to God; he detonated the bomb a fraction of a second too late. The detonation blew the back of my Humvee up in the air and the bomb blast lit up the inside of the vehicle like it was daytime. Only my two front tires remained on the road. I thank God that he targeted me and not the five-ton cargo trucks behind me in the convoy full to the brim with munitions. That would've been a catastrophic moment and a complete mission failure.

We exercised a technique that got us out of the kill zone; we didn't engage the enemy. Usually, there's an immediate attack by insurgents using small arms right after a bomb or IED was detonated. That's when my crew exercised our motto of "Rubbin' is Racin'." If you don't move out of our way, you'll get moved. Other drivers had to get out of our way or be forcefully pushed out of our way. If you trailed our convoy too close, you would receive one warning. If you did not comply, then your engine would get shut down with machine-gun ammunition. An explosion is a pretty unmistakable act of aggression, and we were not in the mood for any more casualties. Getting those munitions back to our base was the top priority.

We made it to a small outpost where we assessed the damage, checked the loads, and contacted the command. We arrived back at the FOB hours later than what we'd originally planned and were met by what seemed to be the entire battalion. I was just glad to be back with all my guys still in my hands and unharmed. I was even more elated that everyone came out and downloaded the munitions we had brought back. The mechanics even took our vehicles so they could inspect, fix, and refuel them for the next mission. Our first sergeant made sure we had dinner though the dining facility had been closed for hours.

I got my dinner to go because I needed to get alone with God and thank Him. He had again lived up to His Word. The plot the enemy had set up for us was meant to make my wife a widow, but that wasn't God's will. Jesus said in John 10:10, "*The thief cometh not, but for to steal, and to kill, and to destroy: I am come that they might have life, and that they might have it more abundantly."* God also promised us in Psalm 91:15–16 (AMP), *"He shall call upon me, and I will answer him; I will be with him in trouble, I will deliver him and honor him. With long life will I satisfy him and show him My salvation."*

It was clear to me that morning that I would not die in that country or lose a single soldier on my missions. There was still one question I needed an answer to—Why did the soldiers from the other unit get severely injured? The Holy Spirit said, *They refused to submit to your position of authority as the soldiers of your unit did. They stayed outside of grace.*

AN IED MEANT FOR ME: MY PSALM 91 EXPERIENCE

On a separate occasion during the same combat tour to Iraq (2004), I watched up close as five soldiers were killed by a massive IED meant for me. My unit was responsible for patrolling and securing the main supply routes (MSR). I had to outfit, arm, supply, and resupply my unit with all we needed for our missions, and that meant conducting convoys to collect what we needed.

The massive IED exploded along my path less than a quarter of a mile away from our gate. It would've been me as the casualty had the combat team of another unit returning from a mission not come between me and it. They weren't supposed to be coming down our side of the road. That was quite unusual. They were coming back to base as we were going out. At the last moment, seeing this combat team coming toward us head on, my convoy commander directed us to cross the median and drive into the oncoming traffic.

As I came parallel to the lead vehicle of the other combat team, the IED exploded. The lead vehicle of the combat team was hit on the far side from me, which caused my vehicle to be shielded from the explosion. Nonetheless, I felt the blast as I watched their up-armored vehicle get blown straight up into the air and then fall completely apart as it came down. It was as if the blast had melted every nut and bolt of their truck. Five soldiers were trapped inside. We were told to get out of the kill zone, which meant not helping the casualties. It was left to the quick reaction force to respond; it was staged just inside the gate of our base. We continued with our mission; the image of what I had seen became etched in my mind. I can still feel the heat of the blast impacting my face. Minutes afterward I recalled the promises of God to His people, promises of safety and security for those who submit to Him and believe His Word.

So many scriptures of safety and security are in the widely known Psalm 91, which truly is the mecca of what the Father says about the security He has set up for us if we believe in His Word. (Read Psalm 91 in the last pages of this book.) I realized that the convoy commander's order to switch lanes was an act of God fulfilling His Word in my life because I believed and confessed His Word. His Word is the deciding factor in all the situations and circumstances of my life.

His Word is activated in your life by believing it in your heart and confessing it with your mouth.[8] When you do that, there's no situation or circumstance that can overthrow what God has said about you as is said in Romans 10: 9–11.

That if thou shalt confess with thy mouth the Lord Jesus, and shalt believe in thine heart that God hath raised him from the dead, thou shalt be saved. For with the heart man believeth unto righteousness; and with the mouth confession is made unto salvation. For the scripture saith, Whosoever believeth on him shall not be ashamed.

DELIVERED FROM HAY FEVER

I exercised the truth of God's Word concerning my body some time before I left for my first combat deployment. In my church, my pastor taught incessantly on faith. Up until 2003, I had annual bouts with hay fever but was realizing that that was a remnant of the curse operating in my life and that I shouldn't be subject to such aggravation; those who suffer from hay fever know how miserable it can make them. My pastor's teaching of the Word made me acknowledge the importance of being in right standing with God and redeemed from every part of the curse because of my belief in Jesus's death and resurrection.

As I drove to the Wednesday night service during hay fever season, I was so fed up with suffering through those symptoms that I rebuked the spirit of sickness and confessed that I was redeemed from hay fever. I commanded the symptoms to be gone. I declared that I would no longer tolerate it.

During my pastor's delivery of the Word that night, by inspiration of the Holy Spirit (and totally off the subject of the message for that service), he laid the blueprint of how I was to take my deliverance from hay fever. However, everyone knows that there's no known cure for hay fever, only medicine to suppress the symptoms. But I knew that by being obedient to these instructions and believing God's Word, I would see the days of headaches, a runny nose, excessive sneezing, and itchy, swollen eyeballs no more.

After service, I rushed out of the auditorium to get in line and purchase a copy of the message so that I could meditate on it and allow it to build and build in me until that word of truth loomed larger than the physical symptoms I was experiencing. At the point of rebuking the spirit of sickness and commanding the symptoms to be gone from my body, I knew I was healed. The only thing left was to see the physical manifestation of my deliverance. What my pastor shared was how to obtain exactly that. He started by reminding us that Jesus was the Word. John 1:1, 14 says,

In the beginning was the Word, and the Word was with God, and the Word was God.

And the Word was made flesh and dwelt among us (and we beheld his glory, the glory as of the only begotten of the Father) full of grace and truth.

So wherever you read "the word of the Lord" in the Bible, you can put "Jesus" in its place.[9]

Then, he read Ephesians 1:19–23.[10]

And what is the exceeding greatness of his power to us-ward who believe, according to the working of his mighty power, Which he wrought in Christ, when he raised him from the dead, and set him at his own right hand in the heavenly places, Far above all principality, and power, and might, and dominion, and every name that is named, not only in this world, but also in that which is to come: And hath put all things under his feet, and gave him to be the head over all things to the church, Which is his body, the fullness of him that filleth all in all.

My pastor made the point that sicknesses had names and that the Word of God, Jesus, had authority over anything that could be named that does not represent or originate from the blessing that God the Father has conferred on you. My pastor had preached these things many times before, but that time was different; he took a more pinpointed approach to how to apply that word to deliberately take deliverance over anything afflicting you in life. He took us to another scripture, where Jesus laid out the blueprint for doing just that.[11]

I read in the Word that if I confessed Him (the Word concerning my deliverance from hay fever) before men, He would confess me before the angels of God. Jesus said in Luke 12:8, *"Also I say unto you, Whosoever shall confess me before men, him shall the Son of man also confess before the angels of God."*

Jesus's confessing us before the angels of God is very significant as they deliver to us what the Word says.[12] Psalm 103:20 says, *"Bless the Lord, ye his angels, that excel in strength, that do his commandments, hearkening unto the voice of his word."*

Hebrews 1:13–14 also helps to clear up the roles of angels.

But to which of the angels said he at any time, sit on my right hand, until I make thine enemies thy footstool? Are they not all ministering spirits, sent forth to minister for them who shall be heirs of salvation?

So if we do our part, Jesus will do His part. Jesus is called the Lord over the Sabaoth, the general over the angelic armies of the kingdom of God.[13] Angels are ministering spirits sent by God to the support of those who are in Christ. These angels hearken to His

Word. My pastor reminded us that the Word of God on earth does not have a voice unless we give it a voice by confessing it before men and thus exercising God's blueprint of deliverance.[14]

Though the hay fever symptoms seemed to become harder to bear, I knew I was putting more pressure on them than they were on me, so the joy surrounding my deliverance increased with each day. But the day came when someone at the office overheard me sneeze about six times in a row, blow my nose, then joyfully give glory to God for the fact that I was free from hay fever. That person asked, "Why do you thank God that you don't have hay fever when you clearly have all the symptoms of it?" I was excited for the chance to confess the Word before men. I shared what the Word of God said by laying out the blueprint. As I did, I felt every symptom come out of my head and chest in a matter of seconds; it was as if I'd never had hay fever. I was whole again, and acting on my faith in God's Word had done that. I went from the hopelessness of having hay fever for the rest of my life to never having another symptom from that moment on.

As I reflected on taking my deliverance from hay fever, my faith, trust, and confidence in God and His Word skyrocketed. It's not only weapons designed to kill that satan uses against you; he comes to steal, kill, and destroy.[16] You've probably never heard of anyone dying of hay fever, but it sure steals your energy, joy, and peace for a season. Because of God's Word, my energy, joy, and peace were restored to me. Satan had been using hay fever to steal from me for years, but I found out the truth and became outraged enough to take my rightful place in authority over it.

God's Word made me speak in defiance of the unhealthy performance of my body. All believers must ask themselves, *Do I know and believe God's Word concerning my situation?* Doubting in your mind is of no consequence when the belief factor in your heart is settled. When you allow doubt into your heart about the truth of God's Word concerning your situation, it thwarts the outcome of what you've declared in faith. That's why I meditated on the scriptures my pastor gave for my deliverance. It kept my mind focused on what the word said instead of the physical symptoms I was experiencing.

Time and time again, I have seen the Word of God become a fact in my life. In every instance, it was because I had deliberately chosen to believe His Word and confess it with my mouth. Then I would speak only what He said concerning the situation or circumstance I was facing and never change my confession. Everything that existed at the time that was contrary to my confession would eventually dissipate, and all that would remain was the Word of God I had confessed.

Embracing what God says about your situation will cause you to speak as it says in 2 Corinthians 4:13: *"We having the same spirit of faith, according as it is written, I believed, and therefore have I spoken; we also believe, and therefore speak."* But what happens after you speak is something you should understand. Job 22:28 says, *"Thou shalt decree a thing, and it shall be established unto thee: and the light shall shine upon thy ways."* That taught me that the combination of believing and speaking was the key to getting biblical manifestations in my life.

It dawned on me that I already knew how to do that and had been quite effective at doing it but on the negative end of the spectrum. For years, I had spoken what I didn't want into my life. I would think negatively, believe it in my heart as the truth based on my experiences, and then speak it out. That's called cursing yourself. It was ironic that at times when I was ready to curse myself, there was always someone present who would agree with me. I got so good at cursing myself that I began to believe I was a prophet; whatever negative thing I said about my life would actually come to pass. Back then, I didn't realize that the heart/mouth connection was a law like gravity. Jesus hit the nail on the head with it in Matthew 12:34: *"O generation of vipers, how can ye, being evil, speak good things? for out of the abundance of the heart the mouth speaketh."*

When your heart is full of something you believe, it is only natural that you speak it with your mouth. When you speak what you believe, will you be justified or condemned by your words? Do your words help or hurt you? Jesus said in Matthew 12:37, *"For by thy words thou shalt be justified, and by thy words thou shalt be condemned."* Proverbs 18:21 says, *"Death and life are in the power of the tongue: and they that love it shall eat the fruit thereof."* These scriptures have merit; I've learned that through my many trials and errors. What you speak can affect outcomes in your life.

I thank God for putting my pastor and certain other ministers in my path; they helped increase my understanding, caused me to reconstruct my foundational beliefs, and enabled monumental shifts in my life. Before my first deployment, the words of truth concerning so many areas of life were flowing into me like a river, and I immediately applied them all as they came.

CHAPTER 14

NO MORE ARMY: WHAT'S MY MISSION NOW?

In 2016, I felt the unction to ask the Father for confirmation of the peace I had in my heart about retiring. The answer came before I could finish asking Him about it. Many people would be affected negatively by my decision if I didn't plan my departure with wisdom. I was involved in planning some very important command initiatives. My command sergeants major and I had several conversations about someone replacing me a month or two prior to my decision to retire. Because of these command initiatives, he told me to count on being the first sergeant for the entire time I was assigned to the organization. I asked the Father to replace me with someone who could pick up my mantle and take to the next level all He had established in that organization through me.

A couple of months later, my replacement was assigned to my unit but in a different capacity. He was appropriately assigned to his duty position, but the Father had me realize that He sent him to be my replacement. In typical fashion, naysayers came out of the woodwork to discredit him though they had no clue that I was planning to retire and that God had chosen him to replace me.

That had always been my way of knowing I was looking in the right direction or doing the right thing especially when it came to selecting people to partner or build a team with.

I observed how that NCO operated and got an idea of his professional ethics and where he stood morally. I couldn't have been more at peace with God's choice. So at the next hail and farewell function, I pulled him and his wife aside and told them I'd decided to retire and asked him if he would replace me as the first sergeant. He said he would.

The first sergeant's position is probably one of the most coveted assignments an NCO could be assigned to. Besides my wife, they were the first people to know I would retire. I told him I'd devise a plan for succession that would maintain the unit's momentum. I controlled the release of information, and the transition was seamless because he was God's choice, not mine. So others could see the wisdom of this move, I gave him a series of tasks and missions that through collaborative planning and solid execution made his capabilities apparent to everyone. I announced my retirement. The new first sergeant was installed, and I started gaining closure on my three-decade career.

One of my biggest questions was exactly how to close out a career that had taken every bit of thirty years to build. As time got closer to my official retirement date, I experienced thoughts and feelings I was unprepared for. I was leaving the army, an environment in which I had become a man. I called that atmosphere normal because I had been a soldier longer than a private citizen. I had been a professional at soldiering and had a limited understanding about civilian life. I thought that the mandatory transition classes would catch me up about civilian life, but that didn't happen. I felt like a fish out of water even before my official retirement.

I still get calls and texts from soldiers around the world who share with me their newest achievements and express their gratitude for things I did that had enabled them to do what they had done or were doing. Such calls remind me that I have been created for positively impacting people's lives and making a difference in this world. God built me up to be a blessing![2] Helping others find their way and achieve real, life-changing success is very satisfying. Seeing people grow, increase, and become their best fills my heart with joy and gives God the glory for what He has done with me and will do through me.

During the last eight months leading up to retirement, I wondered what my place in the world would be. The military offered me nonstop challenges and goals, and I loved that. But out in the civilian world, every opportunity I looked at did not offer anything but a paycheck and a temporary learning curve. Those learning challenges weren't very enticing at all considering how the military had taught me to quickly learn how to do anything; we called it drinking from a water hose.

The job descriptions I perused also left out fighting the enemy, helping others, and saving the world from tyranny. They were all just jobs. None of them applied purpose to my abilities as the military had. The military was also where I learned that I was more than the sum of my abilities. So I knew that keeping my hope and trust in God for my purpose was paramount for a successful transition to my next journey in life.

The months leading up to my official retirement were filled with surgery and recovery, hospital visits, daily physical therapy sessions, soul searching, Bible study, and prayer. I knew for years that my body wasn't 100 percent healthy; I don't know anyone involved in combat arms duty or closely involved with it who could actually maintain a health status above 90 percent; the physical performance requirements for being a paratrooper alone wouldn't allow it.

After I relinquished the diamond (my first sergeant position) for the first time in over twenty years, I was the only soldier I needed to be responsible for. As I looked at my x-rays and data charts from the doctors, I had to acknowledge that my health had to be my top priority. Of course, I was aware of the multiple injuries I had incurred during my many combat deployments and three decades of high-intensity training, but I didn't realize how they had created the compound issues that would cause me to need surgery and daily physical therapy. Through it all, however, God was walking with me down the path He had prepared for me. At times, I thought I was going it alone, but I remembered what He had promised me—that He would never leave me or abandon me. He said it in Joshua 1:5: *"There shall not any man be able to stand before thee all the days of thy life: as I was with Moses, so I will be with thee: I will not fail thee, nor forsake thee."* So I reminded myself that I was never alone and that I would be okay because I was following the path He had laid out for me not a path I created using my own finite wisdom.

THE FAITH JOURNEY TO WACO, TEXAS

His path led us to pack up all we owned and move from our final duty station at Joint Base Lewis-McChord in Washington to a city and state we had never been to or had any relatives in. But we followed what we called His bread crumbs to Waco, Texas. We didn't know much about Waco, but we knew one thing—That was where we were being sent by the Lord, and He provided exactly what we needed just as He said He would. Here's how it happened.

For about eight months before I retired, He worked in me the will to do it.[4] Philippians 2:13 says, *"For it is God which worketh in you both to will and to do of his good pleasure."*

At first, I thought it was simply a fantasy of the mind. You see, my wife and I had kicked around the idea of living in Texas for years. We are die-hard Dallas Cowboys fans, and we thought it would be cool to live there. When we were stationed in Maryland, we lived just down the road from the Washington Redskins' FedEx Field, and our neighbors were very nice until they saw us hang that Cowboys' flag from our porch.

As we discussed it from time to time, the idea began to have more substance, so I began to pray about it, and we began to receive all sorts of confirmation that it was actually His will for us to move there; we realized that it wasn't just a random thought in our minds but an unctioning.

My wife had a wonderful dream about her late beloved grandmother. It was a very short dream but quite significant. In her dream, her grandmother was getting ready to go to church when my wife stopped her to ask why she was dressed the way she was. Her grandmother was wearing a red skirt, a blue blouse, and a white jacket with her purse hanging from one arm and a Bible with a big, white star on it in her hand. As my wife described her grandmother's attire, the Holy Spirit illumined to me that He was telling my wife (through the use of probably the most trusted agent in her life while she was growing up) that we were hearing from God concerning moving to Texas. I told her that the Holy Spirit had dressed her grandmother up as the state flag of Texas. I believe that was more of a confirmation for me than my wife, but it did cause her to agree with me about moving.

I appreciated the Holy Spirit helping me out with the being in the one-accord thing; it's important to God for a husband and wife to be in agreement in all things, of one accord. In times past, telling my wife things didn't always go over so well, but that time it did.

Once, I was stationed overseas on an unaccompanied tour and was coming to the end of that assignment. I asked the Lord where we would be stationed next, and He said, *Fort Riley, Kansas.* When I heard that, I immediately rejected it. I wanted my family and me to be well traveled and experience what the world had to offer. I had a very short list of places I never wanted to take them or even go myself. The only place on that list was Fort Riley, Kansas. It's a much better place to be assigned now, but then, it could not compete with the perks of our former assignment in Chicago. So yes, I rejected it. I could not believe God would send me to the one place I didn't desire to go. I held that rebuke (even though I had heard Him clearly) until I received the official orders three days later. I was shocked.

What was even more troublesome was that I had to tell my wife where we were going. For the previous two years, I'd been deployed overseas while she had been growing two businesses she started in her hometown. Anticipating her response shivered my timbers. The thought of being assigned to Fort Riley without her, if she decided not to come, was unbearable. I prayed for the exact words to say to her. As plain as day, the Lord said, *Tell her to shut them down.*

I never had a problem giving orders to soldiers or even confronting generals and admirals, but the woman that God had given me? That would be a tough task. I was a bit low on courage, but I knew it was impossible for me to speak with her and not be obedient to the Father. As I awoke the next morning, I began to give God praise for all He has done for me. As I did I remembered my vow to never put anyone or anything above my relationship with Him, not even my wife. My courage came roaring back into me.

I knew He was responsible for preparing her heart to receive whatever He would have me say to her. I called and told her what the Lord had said. I was obedient, but she wasn't happy. I knew not to try to soften what I was told to tell her because I was not instructed to say anything else to her about it.

A few months later, I arrived at my new assignment and simply prepared for her and the boys' arrival without any commitment from her to do what God had said. I got a house on the installation and planned to bring them to Kansas. She, however, was planning to stay there and not shut down her businesses.

The movers packed our household goods and then she and I drove the family to Kansas. She stayed with us for three weeks and then flew back. On her flight back, she had an encounter with the Father. His question to her about her willingness to do His will brought her back around to the same point of decision, and she committed to doing His will. Right after she landed, she called me to tell me of her decision. I needed to hear that, the answer to my prayer. I knew that she desired to do the Father's will and would eventually come around to it, but I prayed that her coming around would not be as a result of anything other than her willingness to put His will first in her life, not because of anything I had said or done to convince or pressure her into it. And praise God, that's what happened.

THE FAITH JOURNEY TO WACO, TEXAS, CONTINUED

"It is God that works in you both to will and to do His good pleasure," as it is stated in Philippians 2:13. After my wife's dream, everything changed. My wife was in line for a promotion that would raise her salary to $120k per year, and there were no other people in line for the position.

For me, coming into retirement, that promotion was to be a real pressure reliever. I would've had the latitude to take my time and really weigh my options or possibly not work at all instead of having to find a job that would make up the difference between active duty and retirement pay. As I prayed for direction and instruction, my wife prayed about what she was to do concerning her impending promotion. She thought that the promotion was what God wanted for her, but knowing her clear instruction to move to Texas caused her to resign from the corporation.[10] Without hesitation, we made God's will ours.

Then the fun began. We took virtual tours through many homes in Texas every day for about a month. We went from having a house built where we were in Washington to looking at comparable houses in Texas. We also looked into having a house built but realized that it would take too long for us; prompt obedience was our mantra. We gave God the glory and thanked Him for what He'd done for us and the direction He'd given us.

The matter of finding a home that could accommodate a family of six was becoming a burden. Over my years of walking by faith, I have found that in situations like that, it normally meant that the Father has a hidden treasure laid up for us. I asked Him to reveal it to us, then I believed that we had received it, and we thanked Him for it. He told me to get a real estate agent, send my wife down there to put her feet on the property, and claim it when He showed it to her. So I did. She went with a list of houses to look at but knew that she would come in contact with the house the Father had set aside for us. Within thirty-six hours of her arrival, the house was revealed and she called me to come in agreement with her for it.[11]

We bought the house and moved to Texas completely by faith trusting that God wanted us there. Every time the Father had led us like that, it happened in a similar fashion. Many people seem to think that doing things by faith is like throwing a dart while blindfolded hoping you hit the target—they call it blind faith. But walking by faith is not done blindly. It is deliberately doing something while being well informed and fully aware of the outcome to the point of having the confidence to do it. You won't go where you can't see. So in my book, blind faith doesn't work.

FROM FIRST CIVILIAN JOB TO FINISHING GOD'S DIVINE TASK FOR ME

In God's typical fashion, we were out beyond the ledge. We had taken another step of faith by heading for Waco, but we were at peace about that. He made sure we had plenty of confirmation that we were in His will and doing the right thing.

We arrived in Waco on July 3, 2017, two months after my retirement. We took the first two weeks to acclimate ourselves and recover from the 2,200 mile drive. After that, instead of asking Him what He wanted me to do next, I told Him that I needed to work and asked Him to lead me to a job. He told me that I wouldn't find my work in the house. So I went to sleep that night intending to find a job the next day. I didn't know how to job-hunt in Texas, but He guided me as He'd done many times before, and thirty minutes after I left my house, I was sitting in front of two people who dedicated themselves to getting me employed. By lunch the next day, I was blessed with a number of companies wanting to hire me. It was one of the easiest job-hunting experiences I'd ever had. The favor of God was in full force even though that was not His best for me. I gave Him thanks but asked Him to close the doors of opportunity that weren't for me and open wide the door that was for me, and He did.[12] On the day of my decision, the right opportunity was obvious.

His opening and shutting doors is important to me and my family's walk of faith. Because of this, I make confident decisions knowing that He's guiding my steps. Shutting doors of opportunity at my request also eliminates the opportunity for me to get it wrong and find myself in spaces and places I really shouldn't be. At first glance, wrong opportunities can look much better than the right one, and after you commit to a wrong opportunity, you soon discover how badly you got it wrong and start looking for a way out. With God lighting your path, you can charge forward and never break your stride because your path is lit in a world of darkness. Because you can see where you're going, you're confident and at peace and your steps are sure. I walk by faith and let the peace of God rule my heart when I make decisions.

On the third day of my job search, I interviewed for a position that a company wasn't thinking to hire for at the time. I came to the interview in business attire, but when I got there, I realized I was overdressed and stood out in the group of people who had come. Most were interviewing in shorts and T-shirts. Some applicants needed to be interviewed in their native languages. I asked in spite of my charismatic smile and energy, "Father, what am I doing here?" But over the years, being in a relationship with the almighty God has taught me to be prepared to walk in uncommon places and down unpopular paths. He will often send you to places you'd never go if it were up to you. So I didn't walk out. He made sure I was seen by those who had invited me. Once they saw me, they went to work. I knew then to wait and see what the Father had set up for me.

Within ten minutes, I was in an interview with someone the company had hired less than six months before. Being a thirty-year veteran himself, we spoke plainly with each other. He was upfront with me about why the company was having such a hiring frenzy. They were also rebuilding the frontline leadership team to help them get back into the zone of profitability.

Their problem intrigued me. Too many people run from

problems; they're just after paychecks. (Please, no offense to those who desire only a paycheck from their employment.) I considered myself a problem solver; I did my best work in these conditions. A job can get me a paycheck, but solving problems gives me a platform that allows the kingdom of God to operate through me. My gifts and talents can be exercised and enhanced under these conditions, and the challenges set before me gives me the opportunity to rely on the Father for results. Under troubling conditions, I partner with Him for His expected outcomes. I consider problems to be nothing more than opportunities. Solving an organizations problem can also promote you or at the very minimum open a door.

They offered me the opportunity to manage one of their troubled departments, and I told them I'd let them know within three days, but by the time I got to the parking lot, I knew that God had opened this door for me and wanted me to walk through. I went back to the office and signed the offer. My job search in a new state was over in three days. I accepted the second-best salary I was offered. I went to work every day with the goal in mind to help that company reach its goals. And I brought my relationship with God and the Blessing upon my life to bear for them on a daily basis. I also prayed for my boss, the other frontline managers and the employees that worked for me continually. I did not focus on the paycheck; I did what I had always done—pass the money to my wife.

Five months later, I began to feel the pulling I knew all too well; I knew my days with the company were coming to an end. By that time, the company had undergone a massive overhaul. Every aspect of the business was microscopically measured and recalibrated for maximum production output, and we were on schedule. Within seven months, the operation was under control and the new systems, and procedures were firmly established and profit was made for the first time in four years. Again, I asked the Father for my replacement so what He had sent me to that company to do would not be lost, and He told me to resign.

I woke up two weeks later and in prayer asked the Father, "What am I to do now?" As I began to seek Him for the next steps, I entered a season of recovery from what He had me doing at that company. I had helped get that company into a state of productivity and profitability; an easy day was a fifteen-hour day. After I resigned, He instructed me to sleep longer, go to the gym to recover physically, and of course study His Word. I also had medical and other unfinished business to attend to, so I did that as well. It was only after that that He spoke to me concerning my next endeavor. After I felt refreshed and my lingering unfinished business was accomplished, He said this simple statement: "Finish it!" I knew He meant this book.

If you are unctioned by His Spirit, you are empowered beyond measure to do that thing at that time, which is why my wife and I are promptly obedient in those moments. In all my past endeavors, that meant that success would follow the completion of what He had told me to do. So the best use of my time and energy was in doing what He commanded me to do.

The Bible speaks of the benefits of doing what He wants you to do. In many places, He called them commandments, but they're not like the Ten Commandments.[12] What these scriptures are talking about is the benefits of partnering with God. It's His will that He is getting done in the earth through His people. My finishing this book was His will. I am inspired and empowered by my cooperation with Him to put in this book specific experiences that show His glory in and through my life. So by His grace and meticulous guidance, I finished this book.

MY PRAYER

Father God, I turn the use of this book over to you. I bless all who have dared to believe these accounts of your character. I pray that this book provokes, energizes, and catapults the readers' faith walks into realms beyond what I spoke of in this account of my life.

The intent or effect of this book in your lives is between you and Him now.

NOTES

Unless otherwise indicated, all biblical passages are from the King James Version of the Bible.

Chapter 1. In the Beginning

1 Acts 2:38
2 1 Corinthians 12:4–10
3 John 16:13–15
4 Psalm 116:10; 2 Corinthians 4:13

Chapter 2. The Beginning of a Life of Faith

1 Psalm 127:4

Chapter 3. From Death to Life by Using Your Measure of Faith

1 Isaiah 58:6–14
2 Joshua 1:8–9
3 Mark 4:14, 26–32
4 Genesis 1:26–29; Joshua 1:5; Jeremiah 1:17–19; Isaiah 54:17
5 Genesis 12:3; Deuteronomy 20:3–4; Joshua 1:5–9
6 1 Timothy 6:12
7 Mark 11:22–24
8 Genesis 12:1–3, 10–20; 13:1
9 Malachi 3:6
10 Hebrews 10:23

Chapter 4. Continuing to Grow from Faith to Faith

1 Romans 10:13

2   Psalm 91:11, 12; Hebrews 1:13–14

Chapter 5. The Lost Year

Chapter 6. Rock Bottom

1   Romans 10:13

Chapter 7. Our Challenges Began

1   Romans 10:13
2   Psalm 91:15

Chapter 8. Promotion: God's Way

1   Philippians 4:6–7
2   Peter 5:7; Psalm 55:22
3   Psalm 75:6
4   Proverbs 21:1
5   John 15:20; Matthew 10:17; Romans 8:35–39; 2 Timothy 3:11
6   Matthew 6:33
7   Psalm 37:4–5
8   John 15:7
9   Romans 8:31
10   Genesis 12:2
11   1 John 4:16
12   Matthew 12:34–37

Chapter 9. My Leadership 101

1   Genesis 12:2–3

Chapter 10. Military Leadership 201

Chapter 11. Learning to Walk in Love

1   Luke 6:27–31
2   Luke 10:19
3   Isaiah 54:17
4   Genesis 12:3; Joshua 1:5
5   Deuteronomy 28:7
6   Hebrews 10:30

7   Hebrews 10:23
8   Luke 23:34
9   Romans 12:1
10   Isaiah 54:17; Luke 10:19

Chapter 12. Weaponizing My Love Walk

1   Matthew 5:44
2   1 John 4:8, 16
3   Joshua 1:5
4   Deuteronomy 20:4 AMP
5   2 Corinthians 2:14
6   Matthew 18:7; Romans 16:17; 2 Corinthians 6:3–7
7   Gen 12:3
8   Ezekiel 22:30
9   Proverbs 16:7
10   Ephesians 2:2
11   Romans 8:27–31 (AMP)
12   1 Timothy 2:4; 2 Peter 3:9; Ezekiel 33:11
13   Genesis 1:26–28
14   1 John 4:16
15   Proverbs 31:10–31; Ephesian 5:25, 28, 31; Colossians 3:19; 1 Peter 3:7
16   1 Corinthians 1:27
17   Psalm 103:19; Psalm 75:7
18   2 Timothy 3:13
19   John 4:24; 2 Corinthians 10:4

Chapter 13. The Deployments Were God's Will

1   Job 38:12–13; Psalm 91
2   Matthew 18:18
3   1 Timothy 2:1–4
4   Isaiah 54:17
5   John 10:27–29
6   Psalm 23:1
7   1 Corinthians 1:28–29; Romans 12:1
8   Romans 10:9–10
9   John 1:1–14
10   Ephesians 1:19–22
11   Luke 12:8

12 Hebrews 1:13–14; Psalm 103:19–21
13 James 5:4
14 2 Corinthians 5:20; Luke 12:8
15 Isaiah 54:17
16 John 10:10
17 Mark 11:22–24
18 2 Corinthians 4:13
19 Job 22:28
20 Matthew 12:34
21 Proverbs 18:21
22 Matthew 15:13

Chapter 14. No More Army: What's My Mission Now?

1 Matthew 18:19
2 Leviticus 26:1–13; Deuteronomy 28:1–14

THE SECURITY OF
THE GODLY

He who dwells in the secret place of the Most High shall remain stable *and* fixed under the shadow of the Almighty [Whose power no foe can withstand]. I will say of the Lord, He is my Refuge and my Fortress, my God; on Him I ean *and* rely, *and* in Him I [confidently] trust!

For [then] He will deliver you from the snare of the fowler and from the deadly pestilence. [Then] He will cover you with His pinions, and under His wings shall you trust *and* find refuge; His truth *and* His faithfulness are a shield and a buckler. You shall not be afraid of the terror of the night, nor of the arrow (the evil plots and slanders of the wicked) that flies by day, Nor of the pestilence that stalks in darkness, nor of the destruction *and* sudden death that surprise *and* lay waste at noonday.

A thousand may fall at your side, and ten thousand at your right hand, but it shall not come near you. Only a spectator shall you be [yourself inaccessible in the secret place of the Most High] as you witness the reward of the wicked.

Because you have made the Lord your refuge, and the Most High your dwelling place, There shall no evil befall you, nor any plague *or* calamity come near your tent. For He will give His angels [especial] charge over you to accompany *and* defend *and* preserve you in all your ways [of obedience and service].

They shall bear you up on their hands, lest you dash your foot against a stone. You shall tread upon the lion and adder; the young lion and the serpent shall you trample underfoot. Because he has set his love upon Me, therefore will I deliver him; I will set him on high, because he knows *and* understands My name [has a personal knowledge of My mercy, love, and kindness—trusts and relies on Me, knowing I will never forsake him, no, never].

He shall call upon Me, and I will answer him; I will be with him in trouble, I will deliver him and honor him. With long life will I satisfy him and show him My salvation.

Printed in the United States
by Baker & Taylor Publisher Services